Walking Trails
of Eastern and Central Wisconsin

Bob Crawford

The University of Wisconsin Press
A North Coast Book

The University of Wisconsin Press
2537 Daniels Street
Madison, Wisconsin 53718

3 Henrietta Street
London WC2E 8LU, England

1 2 3 4 5 6 7 8 9 10

Printed in the United States of America

Library of Congress Cataloging-in-Publication Data
Crawford, Robert F., 1935–
Walking Trails of Eastern and Central Wisconsin/
Bob Crawford.
290 pp.   cm.
"A North Coast book."
Includes index.
ISBN 0-299-15574-9 (pbk.: alk. paper)
1. Hiking—Wisconsin—Guidebooks.   2. Trails—Wisconsin—
Guidebooks.   3. Wisconsin—Guidebooks.   I. Title.
GV191.42.W6C73   1997
796.51'09775—dc21   97-6432

For Garrett, Katelyn, Jenny, Hannah, Alec, and Jilianne

Contents

Outagamie County

Winnebago County

Lake Michigan

Door County

Washington County

Waukesha County

Dodge County

North Central

Portage County

Acknowledgments

I don't live in eastern or central Wisconsin, so, while gathering information for this book, I depended upon the help of many people who do live or work there. Without exception the people I talked to, who are familiar with parks and trails described here, were eager to answer my questions.

Superintendents and staff members of state parks, forests, and preserves and other Department of Natural Resources people who helped were William Volkert, Horicon Marsh Wildlife Area; Rodger Reif, Kettle Moraine State Forest; Dave Kleman, Point Beach State Forest; James Bucholz, Kohler-Andrae State Park; Joe Stecker-Kochanski and Tom Renard, Buckhorn State Park; Merle Lang and Lea Bousely, Hartman Creek State Park; Allen Miller, Whitefish Dunes State Park; Kirby Foss, Newport State Park; Marcia Peeters, Peninsula State Park; Jim Rogers, High Cliff State Park; Kent Harrison, Potawatomi State Park; and Mark Martin of the Natural Areas Section, Bureau of Endangered Resources.

In my search for out-of-the-way, little-known trails, I talked to many county park department managers and staff people. Some of the trails they told me about were little known; others were very popular. Especially helpful were Mike Dempske, Manitowoc County; Dale Dorow, Juneau County; Gary Speckman, Portage County; Bill Ehlenbeck, Dodge County; Jim Anderson, Christopher Brandt, and Brian Feest, Outagamie County; Robert Lohry, Winnebago County; Larry Francis, Wood County; Joan Voight, Waushara County; Larry Kascht, Waukesha County; and Ty Baumann, Brown County.

I've included some trail locations in cities that are under the jurisdiction of city parks departments. Paul Meyer and David Kuckuk, in Sheboygan, and Randy Albright, in Manitowoc, helped me with them.

Eastern and central Wisconsin are especially blessed with many private nature centers, and their trails range from wild and rustic to developed and well maintained. For information about these, I thank Bernard Brouchoud, Woodland Dunes Nature Center; Ron Zimmerman, Schmeeckle Reserve; Mike Brandel, Gordon Bubolz Nature Preserve; Paul Regnier, the Ridges

Sanctuary; Ron Zahringer, Ledge View Nature Center; Mary O'Conner, Brillion Wildlife Area; and Mary Holleback, Riveredge Nature Center.

Others who were especially helpful include Kate Harrington of The Nature Conservancy; Andrew Boettcher of the John E. Alexander South Wood YMCA; Elaine Reetz, a Fox River valley historian and author; Christine Thisted of the Ice Age National Scenic Park and Trail Foundation; Kris Kronenberg of the Schlitz Audubon Center; Roy Menzel of the Green Circle Committee; Virginia Seaholm of the Friends of the Recreational Trail; and Dennis Block, Jerry Zeiger, and Bob Stodola, who knew about the West Bend segment of the Ice Age National Scenic Trail.

Last, I would like to remind readers that it is volunteers who have built and maintained many of the wonderful trails in Wisconsin. They work for such organizations as the Ice Age Park and Trail Foundation, The Nature Conservancy, the Sierra Club, and "friends" organizations for state parks and private nature centers. Hikers in Wisconsin owe these unnamed workers their special gratitude.

Introduction

Not long ago I was privileged to be able to hike the Los Angeles Cloud Forest, a private preserve in Costa Rica. A cloud forest is a rain forest on a mountain high enough to be frequently engulfed by clouds. While negotiating a root-laced path I heard a familiar gurgling bird song in the distance. "A house wren," said José, our guide. "He's also a winter visitor from North America." I marveled that I had often heard this same song (could it even have been the same bird?) while walking through Wisconsin woodlands.

I'm not a naturalist, but I find that one of the truly pleasurable things about hiking trails through woods and meadows of the state is the abundant variety that nature displays. Birds that have migrated thousands of miles and plant species that have survived thousands of years (thanks to recent restoration efforts) surround me. And this cornucopia for the senses changes with each season. The frenzied sounds of birds and frogs seeking mates in spring, the rainbow array of prairie wildflowers in summer, the unabashed gaudiness of maples, aspens, and birches in fall, the snow-blanketed silence of winter, all add to the hiker's delight.

I've described in this book more than 200 walking trails in 22 counties composing five regions. You'll find many of the trails in developed parks, forests, and nature centers. I've also included a few quiet paths away from the crowds in remote woods, preserves, or small parks. And I've sprinkled in some walks in urban areas, usually emphasizing history and architecture that I've found along the way.

Because it takes several years to write and produce a book, some of the information here will be out of date upon publication. Please write the University of Wisconsin Press about variances you experience to help us update future editions.

The rating system

I've rated the difficulty of each trail or walking place from one to five, as illustrated by the number of shoes. Lower numbers indicate easier walking. For those trails I haven't walked myself, I've depended upon the judgment of persons familiar with them. Although the system is highly subjective, I've tried to take into account the amount of grade or slope, paving or lack of it, width, possible muddiness or slipperiness in wet weather, clarity of signs or markings, and general maintenance. I think you'll find my ratings to be conservative. An especially physically fit walker will experience less difficulty on many trails than my ratings imply. I've tried to gauge difficulty for the hiker of average endurance, like myself.

Fox Valley

The land owns us,
not the other way round.
We are walking on eternal ground.
The squirrel stores nuts
in the rotting floor.
Man walks his moment
and then
no more.

George Vukelich, from WISCONSIN RUSTIC ROADS

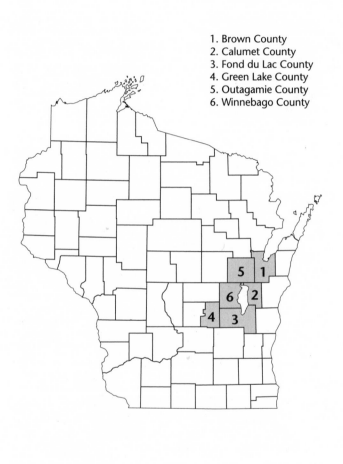

1. Brown County
2. Calumet County
3. Fond du Lac County
4. Green Lake County
5. Outagamie County
6. Winnebago County

Brown County

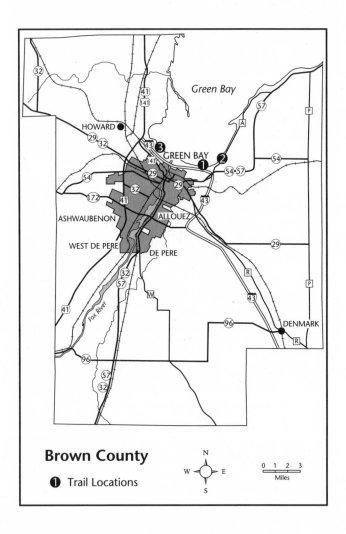

Brown County

1 Trail Locations

N
W — E
S

0 1 2 3
Miles

1 Spend the Day to Appreciate This Urban Sanctuary

Bay Beach Wildlife Sanctuary, Green Bay

When you walk the trails of this urban wildlife facility, plan to spend the day. It will take at least that long to take in all its attractions. You may want to stroll along the border of the deer yard and watch fawns browsing, or try to spot wolves through the fence of the timber wolf habitat. Stops at the Nature Center and the new Woodland Building are a must, but don't forget the Observation Building and the duck shack.

Description and special features. Six miles of trails lace the 700-acre property. Their variety defies description. There are boardwalks through bottomland, asphalt walkways along lagoons, remote paths through forests, a self-guiding nature trail, a habitat demonstration trail, and others. Several highlights follow:

The Hussong Memorial Trail, a 0.7-mile, self-guiding nature trail, keyed to a printed guide, takes the walker through marsh, swamp, forest, and old field. Obtain the guide at the Nature Center for a small fee.

The Chipmunk Trail, a 0.2-mile boardwalk, goes through a sometimes partly flooded swamp.

The Raccoon Trail, the longest at 1.9 miles, extends to the far reaches of the sanctuary through heavy woods. For an even longer hike, a spur of this trail connects to 6 miles of trails in the University of Wisconsin–Green Bay Cofrin Arboretum.

Degree of difficulty. While trail surfacing varies widely, the rolling terrain ensures that none of the sanctuary's trails is extremely difficult to hike. Some may be muddy in wet weather.

How to get there. Bay Beach Wildlife Sanctuary is located along East Shore Drive on the northern edge of the city of Green Bay. From I-43 exit 187, go northeast on East Shore Drive about a quarter of a mile to the entrance on the right. From Green Bay proper take Webster Avenue north. It runs into East Shore Drive.

Regulations. No bicycles, motorized vehicles, or pets are allowed on the trails. Collecting is not permitted. Trails are open daily throughout the year from 8:00 A.M. to 4:30 P.M. The Nature Center hours are: 8:00 A.M. to 8:00 P.M., April 15–September 15; 8:00 A.M. to 5:00 P.M., September 16–April 14. Hours vary on some holidays. Cross-country skiing is allowed on groomed trails.

Facilities. There are restrooms in the Nature Center and the Observation Building. Park near either building or, to hike more remote trails, in a lot along East Shore Drive. The Nature Center and the Woodland Building have a number of unique exhibits of animals in their natural habitats. Exhibits include glass water tanks and a nocturnal-animal viewing area.

Other points of interest in area

Especially for the children, the *Bay Beach Amusement Park* has 13 rides for only 10¢ each. There is a fast-food restaurant and two concession stands, plus picnic shelters. The park is across East Shore Drive from Bay Beach Wildlife Sanctuary on North Irwin Avenue. Phone 414-391-3671 for information.

2 Arboretum Path Encircles University Campus

The Cofrin Arboretum, Green Bay

Students of the environmental sciences at the University of Wisconsin–Green Bay don't have far to go for hands-on experience. The 290-acre Cofrin Arboretum completely surrounds the campus, creating a lush buffer of green on all sides. The university invites walkers to view plant and animal communities from the arboretum's paths.

Description and special features. Two path networks wind through the preserve.

On the **paved path** you can walk a loop entirely around the campus, never leaving the arboretum. Designed for bicycles and joggers as well as walkers, the path follows the forest edge, crosses restored prairie, skirts the university's golf course, and traces a portion of the Green Bay shoreline—a total of more than 4 miles.

The **bark path** goes through most of the woodlands of the arboretum and also traces Mahon Creek and its surrounding bottomlands. A portion of the path follows the Niagara Escarpment, which borders the arboretum on the southeast. An observation tower atop the escarpment provides a panorama of the arboretum, campus, and the waters of Green Bay beyond.

Degree of difficulty. Both paths are uniformly wide and easy to travel. Asphalt or limestone screenings provide a firm surface for the paved path. The bark chips on the bark path have washed away in some areas. The rolling terrain of the property makes path slopes gentle except when descending into the creek valley or ascending the escarpment.

How to get there. The university campus is in the northeast part of the city of Green Bay along Nicolet Drive.

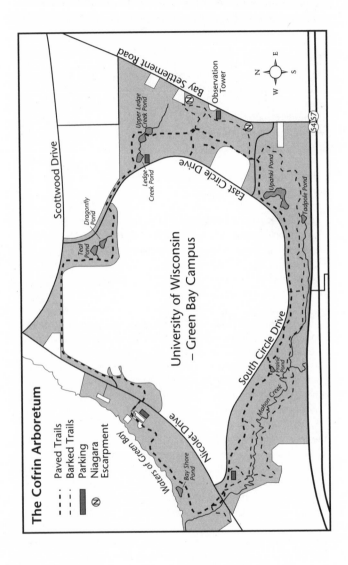

The Cofrin Arboretum

Paved Trails
Barked Trails
Parking
Niagara Escarpment

University of Wisconsin – Green Bay Campus

Scottwood Drive
Bay Settlement Road
Observation Tower
Upper Ledge Creek Pond
Ledge Creek Pond
East Circle Drive
Dragonfly Pond
Teal Pond
Upahki Pond
Tadpole Pond
South Circle Drive
Prairie Pond
Mahon Creek
Nicolet Drive
Bay Shore Pond
Waters of Green Bay
54/57

N
E
S
W

Regulations. Pets, collecting, and motorized vehicles are prohibited in the arboretum. Bikes are permitted on both paths, as is cross-country skiing.

Facilities. You may park in any of four parking lots along Circle Drive, one small lot on Bay Settlement Road near the observation tower, and one off Nicolet Drive near Green Bay.

Other points of interest in area

A mowed path connects arboretum trails to those in *Bay Beach Wildlife Sanctuary* to the southwest (see page 5).

3 Trail Highlights Coastal Wetland Changes

Ken Euers Nature Area, Green Bay

As a memorial to area naturalist Ken Euers, the Green Bay Parks Department preserves this coastal wetland. A printed trail guide titled *A Walk through Time* sketches the natural history of the area, highlighting changes wrought by human habitation. While a walk on the path is a pleasant experience at any time, you'll find it much more illuminating with a copy of the guide in hand. Obtain a copy at Bay Beach Wildlife Sanctuary, 1660 East Shore Drive, Green Bay.

Description and special features. Starting from a parking lot, the 0.8-mile path goes west through the coastal marsh of southwestern Green Bay (the body of water). It then turns south and proceeds along the top of a dike separating the marsh from open water. Looping back to the parking lot it follows a gentle knoll, a former landfill, that overlooks the marsh.

Degree of difficulty. Crushed limestone paves the wide path. The route through the marsh and along the dike is level. The path ascends gently to the crest of the knoll and descends again just before the parking lot. Watch for a few unexpected low tree stumps and animal burrows.

How to get there. The preserve is located at the north end of Military Avenue in the northwest part of the city of Green Bay. From I-43, exit and go north at Atkinson Drive and double back (northwest) on the north frontage road, Hurlbut Street, to Military Avenue.

Regulations. No dogs or motor vehicles are allowed. The trail is closed in April and May to protect nesting birds.

Facilities. There is a large parking lot at the trailhead.

Other points of interest in area

Another large coastal wetland preserve, the *Barkhausen*

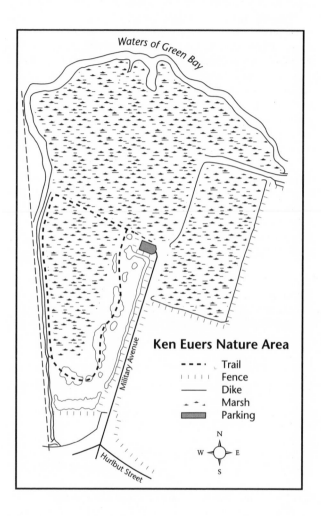

Waters of Green Bay

Ken Euers Nature Area

- - - - Trail
ııııı Fence
——— Dike
▲ ▲ Marsh
▓▓▓ Parking

Military Avenue

Hurlbut Street

N
W ✦ E
S

Waterfowl Preserve, is located a few miles to the north. A system of trails leads the hiker through 950 acres of forest, meadows, marshes, and swamps. The West Shores Interpretive Center in Barkhausen is open daily from 9:00 A.M. to 4:00 P.M. and on weekends from noon to 4:00 P.M. From U.S. 41 in Suamico take Lineville Road 0.4 mile east to Lakeview Drive, then go 0.4 mile north to the entrance on the right.

Calumet County

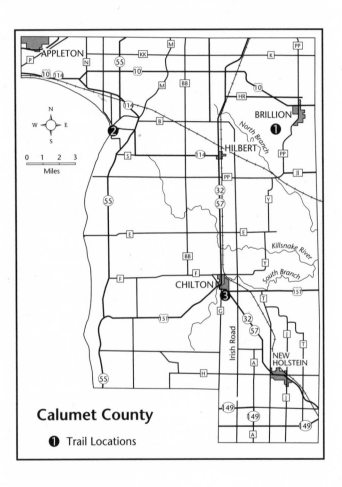

Calumet County

❶ Trail Locations

1 Choose Your Way to Walk This Wildlife Area

Brillion Wildlife Area, Brillion

Bordering Brillion and extending to the west and southwest, the 5,700-acre Brillion Wildlife Area provides a haven for waterfowl, upland birds, and a wide variety of other wildlife. The 2,600-acre Brillion Marsh is surrounded by 800 acres of swamp hardwoods, which are ringed by more than 2,000 acres of upland fields and woodlots.

Within this area, the Brillion Nature Trails volunteer membership association leases 40 acres. On and beyond this property, the association maintains some 8 miles of trails that enable hikers to sample the vast marsh and its surroundings without getting their feet wet.

Description and special features. There are several ways to hike Brillion, depending on your preference. The DNR invites the more adventurous to don waders and experience the marsh close up and personally. An alternative is to walk into the area through any one of several access roads: Bastian Road from the north, or Hilbert Road or Reiner Road from the south.

I prefer the third option, the Brillion Nature Center's hiking trails, because they provide a way to experience not only the marsh, by means of a raised viewing platform, but also the lowland and upland forests with some history and geology thrown in. For example, the Sugar Maple Trail will take you through an abandoned maple syruping operation. The White Oak Trail goes to a limestone pit and rock formations.

The center provided the following list of features of each trail:

White Oak Trail (1.25 miles) goes through upland forest with selective cutting, through lowland forest, and past a limestone pit and formations. The trail connects to Spring Trail and Marsh Boardwalk.

Red Oak Trail (0.5 mile) and **Hickory Trail** (0.66 mile) lead the hiker through upland forest, past a limestone pit and formations and a historic Boy Scout shack.

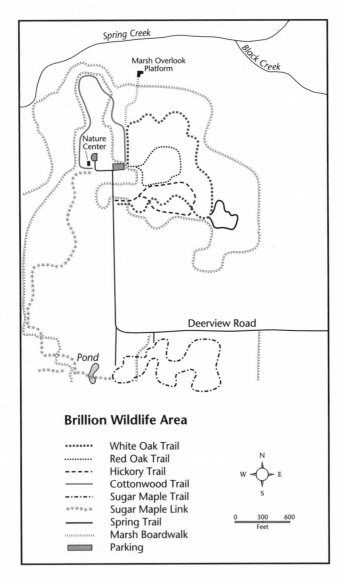

Spring Creek

Black Creek

Marsh Overlook
Platform

Nature
Center

Deerview Road

Pond

Brillion Wildlife Area

········	White Oak Trail
··········	Red Oak Trail
– – – ·	Hickory Trail
———	Cottonwood Trail
–·–·–	Sugar Maple Trail
*****✳*	Sugar Maple Link
———	Spring Trail
⅏⅏⅏⅏⅏⅏	Marsh Boardwalk
▬	Parking

N
W — E
S

0   300   600
Feet

Cottonwood Trail (0.75 mile) includes lowland forest, prairie plantings, and upland forest with selective cutting, and provides access to Marsh Boardwalk.

Sugar Maple Trail (1.25 miles) features upland forest of sugar maples and white pines, a sugar shack, a log building, lime kiln restorations, limestone outcroppings, a picnic area, and views of three ponds.

Sugar Maple Link (1.25 miles) includes a combination of prairie, meadow, and field, a view of marsh ponds, and lowland forest, and provides access to the Sugar Maple Trail.

Spring Trail (0.25 mile) leads the hiker past foundation ruins and a large active spring, through lowland forest, and along a limestone ridge.

Marsh Boardwalk (0.25 mile) transects lowland forest and includes a raised marsh overlook platform and views of Spring and Black creeks.

Degree of difficulty. Except for the Marsh Boardwalk, trail surfaces are natural with some wood chips. Terrain is mostly level.

How to get there. From County PP 2 miles south of downtown Brillion, go west and then north on Deerview Road 1.2 miles.

Regulations. Open 7:00 A.M. to sunset. Dogs must be leashed. All motor vehicles are prohibited on trails. Cross-country skiing is permitted, but trails are not groomed. Bicycles were allowed at this writing but may be prohibited in the future, according to naturalist Mary O'Connor.

Facilities. Pit toilets and parking are available. A nature center with exhibits is open on an occasional basis except in the winter months; when it's open, a part-time naturalist hired by the Brillion Nature Trails Association is present. Knock on the door to see if anyone's there.

Other points of interest in area

Northeast of Brillion near Maribel you can tour a rock mill built in 1847 and listed on the National Register of Historic Places. Tours include the mill, a log house gift shop, and the waterfalls of the Devils River. The mill is at 16612 Manitowoc County R and is open between Memorial and Labor days.

2 Hike the Niagara Escarpment on Four Trails

High Cliff State Park, Sherwood

Over millions of years a limy ooze deposited on an ancient sea bed became a thick layer of limestone. Earth forces tilted this layer downward toward the east so that it formed a huge bedrock saucer. Part of its western edge is a long cliff in Wisconsin. The cliff curves through Michigan's Upper Peninsula and Canada. The saucer's eastern edge protrudes in New York, forming the ledge over which the Niagara Falls flow. That's why the cliff is called the Niagara Escarpment.

Locally known as the ledge, it forms the 223-foot-high backbone of High Cliff State Park. Hike on top of the ledge and enjoy great views of Lake Winnebago. A trail along the side of the ledge reveals the park location's history as a producer of lime.

Description and special features. Each of four hiking trails offers its own unique experience:

Lime-Kiln Trail 👟 👟 👟 👟 (2.3 miles). The trail starts at the site of the ruins of tall stone ovens. These kilns produced lime from 1895 until 1956. Follow the trail southeastward through a state natural area that preserves the unique ecology of the ledge. The trail forms a double loop, returning higher up on the side of the cliff. Its surface is limestone in some places and natural in others. The outgoing trail is usually straight and level, but there are many dips and rises on the return route.

Red Bird Trail 👟 👟 (3.7 miles). This ledge-top trail provides many scenic overlooks of 215-square-mile Lake Winnebago. You can see the cities of Oshkosh, Appleton, Menasha, Neenah, and Kaukauna from various points along the ledge. On the trail, see a 12-foot bronze statue of the Winnebago Indian chief Red Bird, who died a self-imposed death of starvation in 1828 after surrendering himself to the U.S. Army.

The trail goes through an old quarry and connects to the park's other trails. With a mostly natural surface, Red Bird Trail is level except a few slopes in the quarry.

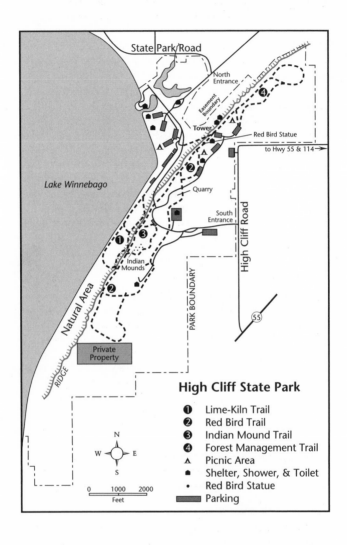

State Park Road

North
Entrance

Easement
Boundary

Tower

Red Bird Statue

to Hwy 55 & 114 →

Lake Winnebago

Quarry

South
Entrance

High Cliff Road

❶

❸

❷

Indian
Mounds

Natural Area

❷

PARK BOUNDARY

55

RIDGE

Private
Property

High Cliff State Park

❶ Lime-Kiln Trail
❷ Red Bird Trail
❸ Indian Mound Trail
❹ Forest Management Trail
▲ Picnic Area
⬟ Shelter, Shower, & Toilet
• Red Bird Statue
▬ Parking

N
W ✦ E
S

0   1000   2000
Feet

Indian Mound Trail 👟 (0.3 mile). Also on top of the ledge, this trail goes among a cluster of mounds built by Early Woodland Indians between A.D. 1000 and 1500. Effigy mounds include four panthers and twin buffaloes. Interpretive signs tell about the mound builders. There is also one scenic overlook of the lake. Surfaced with limestone screenings, the trail is level and easy to walk.

Forest Management Trail 👟 👟 (1.3 miles). Walk through a forest of maple, hickory, oak, and basswood, as well as a restored prairie on this ledge-top trail. Numbered posts are keyed to an interpretive guide that was being developed at the time of this writing. Looping from a parking lot at the northeast end of the park, the trail has a natural surface with a few gentle slopes.

Degree of difficulty. The difficulty varies widely; see the description for each trail.

How to get there. North entrance: From the junction of State Highways 55 and 114, go west 1.1 mile to State Park Road, then south 2.5 miles to the park. South entrance: From State Highway 55, take South High Cliff Road 0.7 mile to the park's entrance on the left.

Regulations. The park is open from 6:00 A.M. to 11:00 P.M. for day users. Dogs are prohibited on trails and must be leashed when elsewhere. Bicycles are permitted only on a portion of the Red Bird Trail, as signs indicate. There is also a separate 8.5-mile trail for bikes and horses. Cross-country skiing is allowed on 4 miles of trails. Users need a state park permit.

Facilities. A full-service state park, High Cliff has camping, picnic shelters, restrooms, a swimming beach, a fishing pond, boat launches, and mooring slips, as well as plenty of parking.

Other points of interest in area

If you're camping and High Cliff is full, which it often is during the summer, *Calumet County Park,* a few miles to the south, also offers camping and hiking on the Niagara Escarpment. The park has a swimming beach, a new bathhouse, playground equipment, and a boat launch. From State Highway 55, take County EE west 1.5 miles into the park. Phone 414-439-1008.

3 Eight Trails Show Off Nature Center's Attractions

Ledge View Nature Center, Chilton

When in 1977 the Calumet County Board of Supervisors bought the "old Zimmerman place," a failed rendering plant south of Chilton, they intended to quarry limestone there. Some ecology-minded citizens steered the board's thinking toward the creation of a nature center. Nearly two decades of development under county naturalist Ron Zahringer have resulted in one of the most well-rounded centers of environmental education and recreation in the area. Some 2.5 miles of trails lead hikers through forests and prairie and even to the site's three caves.

Description and special features. Each of eight separate short trails has its own reason for being. Before your walk be sure to get a copy of the excellent *Nature Trail Guide,* available for a small donation at the exhibit building.

Ledge Walk Trail, the longest at nearly 1 mile, forms a large loop through the 105-acre property and serves as a connector to other trails. Caves named Carolyn's Caverns and Montgomery Cave are on spurs of this trail.

Forest Lane Trail goes through woods of maple, oak, basswood, and hickory, and leads to Mother's Cave and a north-facing ledge with its own microclimate. The trail also goes by the site of the rendering plant that once occupied the property.

Edge Walk Trail highlights the special habitat opportunities the forest's edge provides for wildlife.

Prairie Trail transects a restored prairie. Enjoy a wider view from a 60-foot observation tower on the trail.

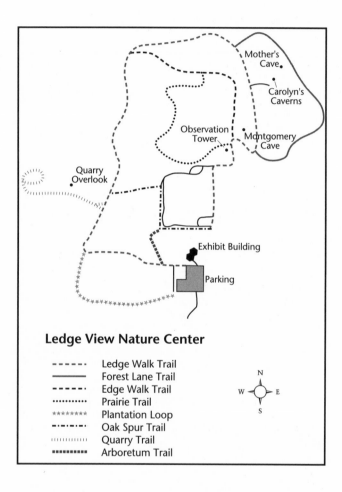

Ledge View Nature Center

- - - - -	Ledge Walk Trail
————	Forest Lane Trail
- - - - ·	Edge Walk Trail
···········	Prairie Trail
********	Plantation Loop
-··-··-··-	Oak Spur Trail
ⅰⅰⅰⅰⅰⅰⅰⅰ	Quarry Trail
▬▬▬▬▬	Arboretum Trail

Labels on map: Mother's Cave, Carolyn's Caverns, Montgomery Cave, Observation Tower, Quarry Overlook, Exhibit Building, Parking

N
W ⊕ E
S

Plantation Loop goes around a spruce plantation and leads to an amphitheater and the sugar bush, where maple syruping is done in late March and early April.

Oak Spur Trail leads from the Arboretum Trail to a forest management plot on the Ledge Walk Trail.

Quarry Trail is a spur with an overview of exposed bedrock in an old quarry. Two information stations provide facts about the geology of the quarry and the Niagara Escarpment, or "the ledge."

Arboretum Trail, the center's newest, was being developed at this writing. Many species of trees and shrubs will be identified along the trail.

Degree of difficulty. Trails have a natural surface and most are on level or gently sloping terrain. The Forest Lane Trail descends into a lower area with a few steeper inclines.

How to get there. From its junction with U.S. Highway 151 in Chilton, take County G south 0.6 mile to Short Road, then east 0.2 mile to the center's entrance on the left.

Regulations. Trails are open from sunrise to sunset. The exhibit building's hours are 8:00 A.M. to 4:30 P.M. Tuesday through Friday, 10:00 A.M. to 4:30 P.M. Saturday and Sunday, closed Monday. Pets must be leashed. No bicycles or motor vehicles are allowed. Cross-country skiing is permitted.

Facilities. There are restrooms separate from the exhibit building and parking nearby. The exhibit building has displays of mounted animals, a fish tank, and other nature exhibits. A live red-tailed hawk and a great horned owl occupy exhibit cages in a separate building.

Other points of interest in area

For a special adventure, take a guided tour of the site's three caves. Tours are held throughout the year. A descent into Mother's Cave, called the adventure cave, involves climbing down about 7 feet, lying down and crawling through "the squeeze," and going about 150 feet up and over rocks. For dates and times, call the center at 414-849-7094.

Fond du Lac County

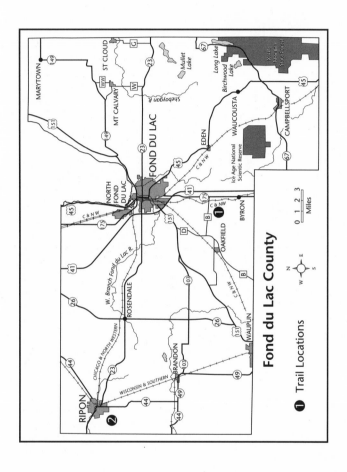

Fond du Lac County

1 Trail Locations

0 1 2 3
Miles

1 Trails Follow Creek through Climax Hardwood Forest

Hobbs Woods Nature Area, south of Fond du Lac

Gently flowing Parson's Creek meanders through a deep glen that contains a climax hardwood forest where sugar maples, oaks, and basswoods dominate. This forest represents the last phase of the cycle that forests go through during a 200–300-year period. The glen of this 60-acre Fond du Lac County park provides habitat for a rich variety of wildlife. More than 100 bird species have been sighted here.

Description and special features. A much larger river than the present-day Parson's Creek carried glacial meltwater some 10 or more centuries ago. Its torrent cut a deep glen with a wide bottom, through which Parson's Creek now flows. The trails of Hobbs Woods follow both sides of the creek, close to its banks, as well as the rim of the valley.

From a small parking lot, the 0.75-mile nature trail goes along one side of the creek, crosses it, and returns on the other side. Sixteen numbered posts, keyed to a printed guide, identify features of the mature forest, wildlife habitat, and characteristics of the valley. (Obtain copies of the guide from the County's Planning and Parks Department, on the fourth floor of the City-County Government Building, 160 South Macy in Fond du Lac.)

Other trails weave throughout the forest in the lower valley and oak savannah of upper portions, covering the entire 60 acres.

Degree of difficulty. Constructed by the Youth Conservation Corps and members of the Fond du Lac Audubon Society, the trails are mostly level but include a few steep sections going from the lower glen to its rim. Wooden steps make the going easier in one especially steep portion. Wide wooden-plank bridges span the stream at more heavily used crossings, and large stepping stones are provided in a few places.

I found some lower portions of the trail, mostly shaded under

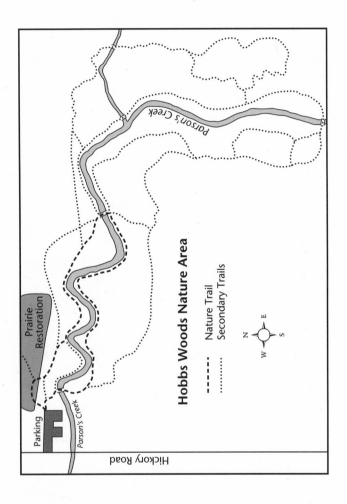

Hobbs Woods Nature Area

- - - - - Nature Trail
·········· Secondary Trails

Prairie Restoration

Parking

Parson's Creek

Parson's Creek

Hickory Road

N
W E
S

the thick canopy of the woods, to be muddy during my April walk, especially where bordering the creek. Tracks revealed that trail bikes had rutted the path and added to the problem. Park personnel have paved many portions of the trail with wood chips to absorb moisture, and a boardwalk crosses some soft bottomland.

The rest of the trail, both in the glen and along the rim, was dry and easy to walk.

How to get there. From the Fond du Lac south city limits on State Highway 175, go south 3.3 miles to County B, then west 1 mile to Hickory Road, then south 0.3 mile to the entrance on the left.

Regulations. Open 6:00 A.M. to 10:00 P.M. Cross-country skiing is permitted.

Facilities. Parking.

Other points of interest in area

Eldorado Marsh, 4 miles west of Fond du Lac on State Highway 23, is a 5,500-acre, state-owned wetland providing habitat for many birds and other wildlife. Drive north from the marsh entrance to either of two parking lots and walk the access roads and dikes.

North Woods Nature Area, an undeveloped county park, has short walking trails going north, east, and south from a small parking lot. Trails stop short of a wetland in the east portion. From State Highway 23 in Rosendale, go north on State Highway 26 2.3 miles to the parking lot on the right.

2 Rustic Trail Meanders through Stream Valley

South Woods Nature Study Area, Ripon

On the edge of the bustling college town of Ripon, this preserve offers a true backwoods hiking experience.

Description and special features. From a parking lot a trail gently descends into this privately owned valley of Crystal Creek. On a trail that branches off to the left, you can follow the bank of the creek to the south end of the preserve. Or go straight and take a loop through the north portion, which crosses the creek and ascends the high west wall of the valley. This portion of the trail then returns to the creek, crosses it again, and rejoins the entry trail.

The trail goes through a mature, mostly oak forest. The narrow creek meanders through a wide, deep valley, which obviously carried a much larger volume of water during early postglacial times.

The South Woods Park Association invites your membership. To help maintain the preserve, send $5 to the association at P.O. Box 441, Ripon, WI 54971.

Degree of difficulty. A variety of characteristics gives the trail a rating of five shoes. While there is one wooden-plank bridge, other stream crossings involve stepping stones. The trail ascends the steep valley wall almost directly in one place. Unsurfaced, the trail is muddy during damp weather, especially near the creek. Deadfall trees crossed the path in several places when I hiked here. A portion of the trail closely follows the edge of the steep valley wall. These are not criticisms of the trail; the purpose of this area is nature study, and the park association is trying to preserve its natural state.

Though prohibition of trail bike use is posted at the trailhead, I observed during my spring walk that they had caused deep ruts in low, damp portions of the trail. (I saw seven trail bikers during my 1-hour walk.)

How to get there. To find the park, just southwest of Ripon, take Union Street south from the city limits 0.2 mile. There's a small parking lot on the right at the trailhead.

Regulations. Open daily from 6:00 A.M. to 10:00 P.M. Leashed pets are allowed.

Facilities. Parking only.

Other points of interest in area

Ripon has *three recreational trails,* mostly following former railroad beds. A 1-mile trail goes from Pacific Street just north of the public library to beyond Oshkosh Street. Plans call for the trail eventually to extend several more miles to the Green Lake County line.

A second walking-biking trail starts off Locust Road near County E north of Ripon and runs several miles to Green Lake County.

The 0.25-mile Kiwanis Trail from Thomas Street leads to a meadow and a ski hill.

Three self-guiding historic walking tours will take you by many nineteenth- and early-twentieth-century homes and other buildings. One tour includes the "Little White Schoolhouse," where the Republican party was formed in 1854. Obtain brochures with maps from the Ripon Area Chamber of Commerce, 301½ Watson Street, and other locations.

Green Lake County

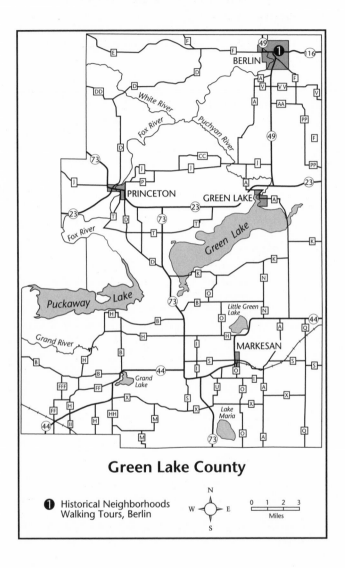

Green Lake County

❶ Historical Neighborhoods
Walking Tours, Berlin

0 1 2 3
Miles

1 Two Walking Tours Showcase Restored Victorian Homes

Historical Neighborhood Walking Tours, Berlin

In the nineteenth century settlers from New England and New York prospered in Berlin's quarrying and cranberry industries. The grand houses they built reflected their back-east tastes. Many of these Victorian-era homes have been meticulously restored. You can view them on two walking tours, described in a brochure produced by a city business organization.

Description and special features. So many present owners of these homes wanted to be included in the tour that the original single tour of about 20 homes has been doubled in size and split into two tours. Homes include examples of Queen Anne, Italianate, Eastlake, Gothic Revival, Colonial Revival, Greek Revival, Romanesque Revival, and others. A park, several churches, and a stone quarry are also shown. A colored plaque identifies each home or building along the way.

You may obtain a brochure with maps and descriptions at many stores in Berlin, including Old Abe Antiques, 133 W. Huron Street. Hours there are 9:00 A.M. to 5:00 P.M. Monday through Saturday, and 10:00 A.M. to 5:00 P.M. Sunday. Guided tours are offered for groups of 10 or more. Call Jim Peterson at 414-361-0889.

Strongsville Tour homes (red plaques) are in a 3-square-block area bordered by Wisconsin Street on the west, Moore Street on the north, State Street on the east, and Park Avenue on the south.

Nathan Strong Park Tour (green plaques) is generally in a 2-square-block area bordered by Oak Street on the west, Park Avenue on the north, Church Street on the east, and Huron Street on the south. In either tour there are homes on both sides of many of the streets.

Degree of difficulty. Both tours follow the sidewalks of residential streets. Terrain is level.

How to get there. Berlin is in northeast Green Lake County at the junction of State Highways 116 and 49.

Regulations. Sponsors request that you view these private properties from the front sidewalk.

Facilities. You may park on the streets as signs indicate.

Other points of interest in area

Fur and leather crafters of Berlin are widely known for their skills. About a half-dozen downtown merchants display their wares, including custom-made shoes, deerskin apparel, wallets, and fur coats.

Outagamie County

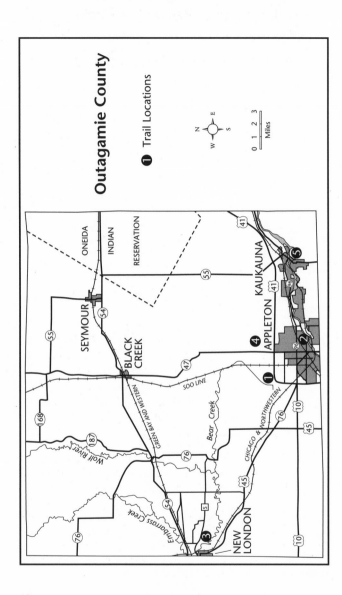

Outagamie County

1 Trail Locations

N
W E
S

0 1 2 3
Miles

ONEIDA

INDIAN

RESERVATION

SEYMOUR

BLACK
CREEK

KAUKAUNA

APPLETON

4

1

2

5

3

NEW
LONDON

SOO LINE

GREEN BAY AND WESTERN

CHICAGO & NORTHWESTERN

Bear Creek

Embarrass Creek

Wolf River

41

55

54

55

47

168

187

76

54

45

76

76

45

10

10

96

41

96

1 Walk a Preserved Remnant of a White Cedar Forest

Gordon Bubolz Nature Preserve, Appleton

If you're planning to visit a nature preserve in the summer, try to do it in the early morning before the crowds and heat shoo the animals into their shady retreats. I arose with the sun on the day of my July visit to the Bubolz Preserve. Rabbits as tame as kittens watched as I passed, and songbirds flitted busily among the dogwoods.

Some of Bubolz's 8 miles of hiking trails go through one of the few remaining remnants of Wisconsin's original 500,000 acres of white cedar forest. Others traverse meadows and restored prairies or skirt ponds. The preserve's 762 acres of prime wild-life habitat offer opportunities for both organized and casual learning about the ecosystem while you enjoy hiking or cross-country skiing.

The nonprofit preserve welcomes donations and offers special benefits to members of its "friends" organization.

Description and special features. Shorter and longer trails provide a variety of experience. Three short trails—**Four Seasons** (0.5 mile), **Esker** (0.4 mile), and **North Bush** (0.1 mile) —are nature trails primarily used for education, according to preserve manager Mike Brandel. Pick up an informative guide at a trailhead dispenser (50¢ donation requested).

The **White Cedar Trail** (1.5 miles) provides a brief sojourn into the forest, while the **Deer Run Trail** (2.5 miles), offers a longer, back-country-like hiking experience into the white cedar swamp.

The **Wilderness Trail** (4 miles) goes through the outer reaches of the preserve. The time it is open is limited—for hiking during the fall and for cross-country skiing in winter—in order to provide a secluded sanctuary for wildlife species during their breeding cycles.

Degree of difficulty. Crushed stone paves the Four Seasons, Esker, North Bush, and White Cedar trails. They are wide and easy to walk. The Deer Run Trail's wood chip surface is narrower in many places and less meticulously maintained. Although the Wilderness Trail was closed during my visit, I'm told it is similar to the Deer Run Trail but may be soggy in wet weather. The terrain of the preserve is generally level. Shorter trails are wheelchair accessible.

How to get there. From the intersection of U.S. Highway 41 and County OO in northwest Appleton, go east 1 mile to County A and north 1.5 miles to the preserve's entrance road on the left.

Regulations. Trails are open daily from dawn to dusk. The earth-shelter nature center building hours are 8:00 A.M. to 4:30 P.M. Tuesday through Saturday, and 12:30 to 4:30 P.M. Sunday. The building is closed Mondays and holidays, and it may be closed for short periods other days when staff members are in the field (phone 414-731-6041). Neither pets nor bicycles are allowed. Cross-country skiing is permitted.

Facilities. There are restrooms in the nature center as well as a small retail shop, exhibits, and an auditorium. The preserve has a small amphitheater for organized outdoor programs, a picnic area, a trout pond with a wheelchair platform, and two rental cabins for meetings.

Other points of interest in area

The *Fox Cities Children's Museum* provides hands-on exploration and discovery for children and adults. Educational exhibits and programing emphasize participatory learning. In Appleton's Avenue Mall at 10 College Avenue, the museum is open daily except on major holidays and requires an admission fee.

2 Illusionist's Haunts Retraced on Walking Tour

Houdini Historic Walking Tour, Appleton

Harry Houdini, illusionist, escape artist, and debunker of occult fraud, grew up in what is now downtown Appleton. Places where he lived, frequented, and performed his magic are now memorialized in a 15-stop walking tour. Though most of the original buildings have been replaced, brass plaques trace the highlights of his life in Appleton.

Description and special features. Except for a location on the Fox River where Houdini nearly drowned as a boy, the tour covers a compact, approximately 8-block area in the vicinity of College Avenue. Stops include the master magician's birthplace, a location where he was interviewed by author Edna Ferber, the "official" seance site, places where he performed, and the Houdini Historical Center, described below. A highlight, the *Metamorphosis* sculpture on Houdini Plaza, depicting a box, chain, and lock, symbolizes his many escapes.

Degree of difficulty. The entire tour is on city sidewalks and a plaza. Terrain is level. Busy street crossings are the sole hazard.

How to get there. The bulk of the tour is in downtown Appleton within a block of College Avenue between Superior and Drew streets.

Regulations. A stop on the tour, the Houdini Historical Center, is open the year around Tuesday–Saturday from 10:00 A.M. to 5:00 P.M., and Sunday from noon to 5:00 P.M.

Facilities. Parking is available in one of several nearby ramps or at meters on the street.

Other points of interest in area

The *Houdini Historical Center,* 330 East College Avenue, contains a collection of photographs, documents, posters, and

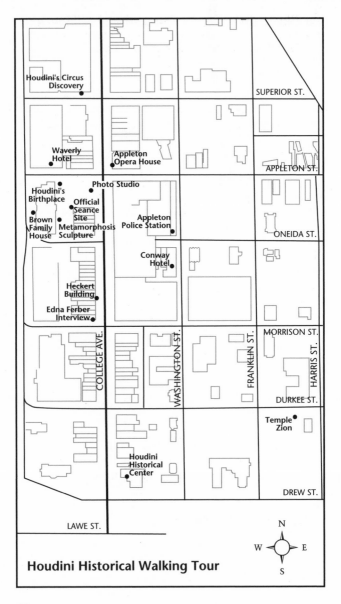

Houdini's Circus
Discovery

SUPERIOR ST.

Waverly
Hotel

Appleton
Opera House

APPLETON ST.

Photo Studio

Houdini's
Birthplace

Official
Seance
Site

Brown
Family
House

Metamorphosis
Sculpture

Appleton
Police Station

ONEIDA ST.

Conway
Hotel

Heckert
Building

Edna Ferber
Interview

COLLEGE AVE.

WASHINGTON ST.

FRANKLIN ST.

MORRISON ST.

HARRIS ST.

DURKEE ST.

Temple
Zion

Houdini
Historical
Center

DREW ST.

LAWE ST.

N

W   E

S

Houdini Historical Walking Tour

handbills about the illusionist. Also on display are leg-irons, lock picks, and handcuffs he used, as well as the Guiteau handcuffs that held President Garfield's assassin and from which Houdini escaped. A fee is charged.

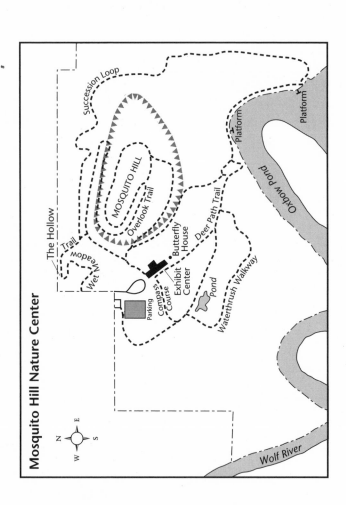

Mosquito Hill Nature Center

The Hollow

Succession Loop

MOSQUITO HILL

Overlook Trail

Wet Meadow Trail

Butterfly House

Deer Path Trail

Exhibit Center

Compass Course

Parking

Pond

Waterthrush Walkway

Platform

Platform

Oxbow Pond

Wolf River

N
E
W
S

3 Nature Center Paths Feature Hill and Ponds

Mosquito Hill Nature Center, New London

The mosquitoes on the Outagamie County hill that is the center piece of a 430-acre nature center are no worse than you might expect in any place in Wisconsin bordered by ponds and a river. But the hiking is superb on the five trails on the hill and through the wetlands.

Description and special features.

Overlook Trail 👟 👟 👟 👟 (1.05 miles) rises 200 feet through deciduous woods to the top of Mosquito Hill. You can take either of two routes to the top. The more direct route is steeper. The trail is wide with a shredded-bark surface.

Deer Path Trail 👟 👟 👟 (0.75 mile) goes through restored prairie to the Oxbow Pond, a remnant channel abandoned by the Wolf River. Two sturdy platforms will take you out over the pond. The trail returns through woods on the side of Mosquito Hill.

Waterthrush Walkway 👟 (0.37 mile) goes through a maple swamp that is part of the Wolf River bottomland. Trail builders elevated the firm, crushed limestone surface to keep your feet dry.

Succession Loop 👟 👟 👟 (1.02 miles) branches off the Deer Path Trail and goes through grasslands. You'll do some moderate climbing as you follow the trail around the base of Mosquito Hill.

Wet Meadow Trail 👟 (0.2 mile) has a hard surface of limestone screenings to accommodate wheelchairs and walkers. It accesses the Hollow, a former gravel pit now used as an amphitheater, and then continues on to an elevated site overlooking the meadow.

Degree of difficulty. All trails are wide and exceptionally well maintained. Surfacing varies to suit the location, from mowed grass or shredded bark to raised limestone paving. The shorter trail up Mosquito Hill is steep. Others have moderate slopes or, as in the case of the Waterthrush Walkway, none.

How to get there. From its junction with State Highway 54 in eastern New London, take County S east 1.65 miles to Rogers Road, then south 0.4 mile to the Exhibit Center.

Regulations. Trails are open daily during daylight hours except during the firearm deer hunting season. Exhibit Center hours are 8:00 A.M. to 4:30 P.M. Tuesday through Friday, and 10:00 A.M. to 3:00 P.M. Saturday and Sunday. The following are prohibited: collecting, camping, bikes or motorized vehicles other than in the parking lot, smoking, radios, horses, dogs, and other pets. Picnicking is permitted on a patio adjacent to the Exhibit Center and in other designated areas.

Facilities. There is a parking lot near the Exhibit Center, and restrooms and water are available inside the center. There are nature exhibits, large meeting rooms, and separate classrooms with theme exhibits about soil, plants, and ponds. The center also has an information counter and a small retail shop. Stop there for a printed trail guide. On the Wet Meadow Trail you'll find a drinking-water pump.

Other points of interest in area

The unique *Butterfly House* near the Exhibit Center houses plants that attract specific species of butterflies. Depending upon the month, you're apt to see a variety of caterpillars and butterflies, some rare, among the cultivated plants and flowers. The screen-walled house is open Wednesday, Saturday, and Sunday from July through the first Sunday in September. Hours are from 11:00 A.M. to 3:00 P.M. Volunteers will provide information.

4 Learn Birding Techniques on Unique County Park Trail

Plamann Park, north of Appleton

The hiking is great in this county park. You'll be challenged by a long trail through meadows and ravines, a shorter nature trail, and even a trail designed to teach the basics of bird watching. But hiking is just one of the many things you can do there. Visit a children's farm to pet live animals, try an 18-hole disk course, or swim in Plamann Lake.

Description and special features

The main **Hiking Trail,** 👟 👟 👟 also used for cross-country skiing, courses throughout the wooded area, which makes up about half of the 257-acre park. Information stations along the way tell about the benefits of walking as exercise.

A highlight of the park, the **Bird Trail,** 👟 teaches the techniques of bird watching by means of information stations along its route over grassy meadows. Spruce trees and bushes provide nesting cover for numerous species of birds. A tree swallow hovering overhead monitored my movements closely as I walked among the spruces, apparently near its nest.

The **Nature Trail** 👟 👟 👟 goes through a climax forest of maples and basswoods. Information stations tell about the forest and its ecology.

The park also has a **Fitness Trail** with Parcourse exercise stations.

Degree of difficulty. The wooded portions of the park, over which the Nature Trail and much of the Hiking Trail go, are especially hilly with ravines running toward Apple Creek. Trails have wood-chip or natural surface and some short but steep slopes. The Bird Trail and the Fitness Trail have gentler inclines and a mowed grassy surface.

How to get there. From its intersection with U.S. Highway 41 just north of Appleton, go north on State Highway 47 for 2 miles to Broadway, and east 1.4 miles to the park entrance on the right.

Regulations. The park is open from dawn to 11:00 P.M. No dogs are allowed.

Facilities. This full-service park has restrooms, picnic shelters, ball diamonds, and the other features mentioned above. There is no camping.

Other points of interest in area

For more advanced birding, visit the *Outagamie State Wildlife Area* to see sandhill cranes, nesting ospreys, cuckoos, black terns, and others. The 690-acre marsh and woodland borders the Wolf River. There are hiking trails on dikes. It's located 2.5 miles north of Shiocton on the east side of County E.

5 Eagles Nest along Nature Center's Riverside Trail

1,000 Islands Environmental Center, Kaukauna

In 1976 the Kaukauna City Council set aside 240 acres along and adjacent to the bank of the Fox River as a conservancy zone. Two years later they authorized construction of the first stage of the 1,000 Islands Environmental Center. Since then miles of hiking paths, including a boardwalk through the Fox's bottomlands, have been built. From the riverside path you may see several varieties of herons, six kinds of ducks, and even eagles in their habitats near the Fox.

Description and special features. The conservancy zone has two major hiking path systems. The riverside path begins near the Environmental Center with several connecting boardwalks going through river bottomlands. They provide a rare chance to see wildlife and vegetation typical of this type of habitat close up. Changing from boardwalk to wood chip surface, the path then follows the river bank, climbing to a scenic view of the lower Fox.

Another maze of paths laces a woods of maples, basswoods, oaks, and hickories in the southern portion of the conservancy zone, south of County Highway Z. Also used for cross-country skiing, these paths are wide and have mostly natural surface.

Degree of difficulty. The riverside path beyond the boardwalks has some slopes and dips but is easy to follow. The woodland paths south of County Z/Dodge Street are wide and on mostly level terrain, with some gentle hills and only a few very steep inclines.

How to get there. The Environmental Center, which is located on the west edge of the conservancy zone, is on County Z (Dodge Street) on the south side of the Fox River near downtown Kaukauna.

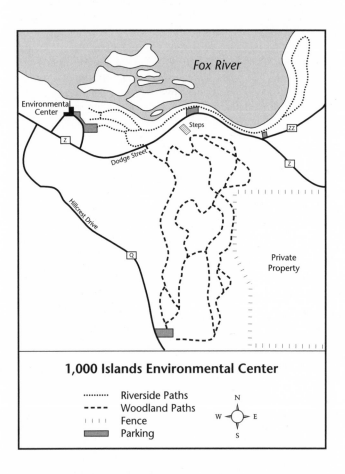

1,000 Islands Environmental Center

··········	Riverside Paths
- - - -	Woodland Paths
ı ı ı ı	Fence
▬	Parking

Regulations. Hiking paths are open during daylight hours. The Environmental Center's hours are 8:00 A.M. to 4:00 P.M. Monday through Friday, and 10:00 A.M. to 3:30 P.M. Saturday and Sunday. It is closed on major holidays. No pets, bicycles, or motor vehicles are allowed on the trails. Cross-country skiing is permitted.

Facilities. There are restrooms in the center and parking nearby.

Other points of interest in area

Inside the Environmental Center is a unique display of mounted African wild animals that have been donated by the estate of a local big game hunter. A lion there is "world class," according to information provided. Also included is a variety of antelope species.

Winnebago County

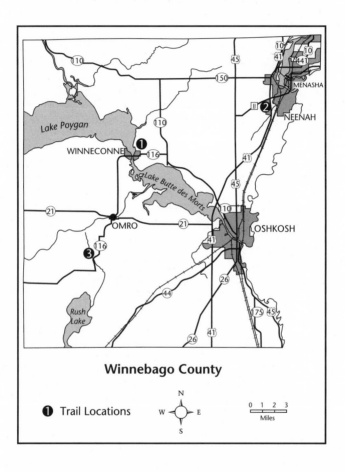

Winnebago County

1 Trail Locations

N
W ⊕ E
S

0 1 2 3
Miles

1 Secluded Trails Lace Ancient Indian Village Site

Lasley Point Archaeological Site, Winneconne

Between A.D. 1200 and 1500 this land supported an Oneota Indian village. Numerous archaeological digs in the 1940s unearthed human bones, bone tools, shells, copper flakes, charcoal, and pottery, as well as early garden beds and cache pits. Winnebago County purchased the site, which is listed on the National Register of Historic Places, in 1981 for preservation and education.

Description and special features. Adjoining trails lace the 47.7-acre property, going through woods of oak, basswood, ash, and many hickories. Most of the trees have grown up since the 1940 activity of archaeologists. Thick underbrush conceals the sites of the digs. In an out-of-the-way rural location, Lasley Point offers a secluded, usually quiet walking experience. (Map is on p. 58.)

Degree of difficulty. Hiking is easy on five numbered, wide paths totaling about 1.5 miles on level, natural turf.

How to get there. From State Highway 116 just east of Winneconne, go north on County M for 1 mile to Lasley Point Road, and west 0.5 mile to a parking lot on the right.

Regulations. Open 6:00 A.M. to 11:00 P.M. No hunting, camping, all-terrain vehicles, or snowmobiles are allowed. Cross-country skiing is permitted.

Facilities. A small parking lot.

Other points of interest in area

Lake Winneconne Park, in the village off Parkway Drive, has restrooms, picnic shelters, playground equipment, horseshoe pits, and an unsupervised swimming beach.

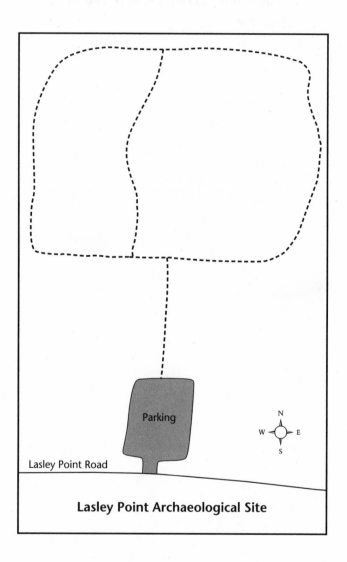

Parking

Lasley Point Road

Lasley Point Archaeological Site

N
W ─◇─ E
S

2 Farmer's Good Deed Preserves Old Woods

Memorial Park, Neenah

When Henry Swatscheno sold his farm to the city of Neenah, he so loved the 20-acre maple woods on the property that he added a proviso to the deed. It stipulated that the woods must remain as a public recreation area dedicated "to all who enjoy nature."

Description and special features. A main trail forms a loop through a forest of maples, basswoods, and a few oaks. The maples are estimated to be more than 100 years old, and the oaks perhaps 150 years. A number of trail spurs and subsidiary loops reach to the edge of the woods. Arrange to take your walk in autumn if you can, to enjoy the typically bright colors of this climax forest.

Degree of difficulty. The wide main trail is surfaced with wood chips. Other, narrower trails have natural surface, all over level terrain. Although only 20 acres in size, the woods are thick enough for walkers to lose their way, especially off the main trail, since there are no guideposts.

How to get there. From its junction with U.S. Highway 41 take County JJ west 0.35 mile to Tular Road, and south 0.6 mile to the park on the right.

Regulations. The park is open 6:00 A.M. to 10:00 P.M. Neither pets nor bikes are allowed on the trails.

Facilities. Restrooms are located near the trailhead. The park has a picnic shelter, playground equipment, and ball fields, as well as a parking lot.

Other points of interest in area

See an outstanding collection of glass paperweights and Germanic glass at the *Bergstrom-Mahler Museum,* 165 North Park

Avenue, Neenah. Hours are 10:00 A.M. to 4:30 P.M. Tuesday through Friday, and 1:00 P.M. to 4:30 P.M. Saturday and Sunday, except major holidays. Admission is free, but donations are appreciated.

3 Nature Trail and Hiking Trail Offer Variety and Challenge

Waukau Creek Nature Preserve, Waukau

North of the village of Waukau, a gentle creek has formed a broad ravine where a variety of deciduous trees, wildflowers, and bottomland plants grow. A network of trails follows the creek and the rim of the ravine, offering both leisurely and strenuous hiking.

Description and special features. From a grassy roadside area, the trail descends into the ravine. The first part is a nature trail with information stations identifying trees and wildlife. This short trail loops back to the road. Branching from it, a back-country hiking trail forms a large loop with several side trails that wind throughout the 64-acre preserve. Trails have a natural surface and vary considerably in width and maintenance.

Degree of difficulty. The nature trail has some gentle, bare slopes that may be slippery when wet. About two-thirds of the back-country trail is wide, though with some steep inclines. A well-built steel and wooden-plank bridge crosses the creek.

During my September walk, I found the farther reaches of the back-country trail in the southern part of the preserve to be overgrown and extremely hard to follow. While trail maps were helpfully located at trail intersections, I found it necessary to ford the stream when I failed to find a bridge indicated on the maps. I followed orange ribbon markers through thick underbrush to find my way back to the road.

How to get there. From County K north of Waukau, take Delhi Road 0.2 miles north to the preserve. Parking is on the left and the trailhead is on the right side of the road.

Regulations. Hunting is prohibited in county parks.

Facilities. Across the road from the trailhead, there are parking, pit and portable toilets, a picnic shelter, and a water pump.

Other points of interest in area

For a stroll through a thriving strip of natural prairie reminiscent of presettlement days, visit The Nature Conservancy's *Omro Prairie.* Some 62 species of prairie plants grow on this former railroad right-of-way, which is 0.5 mile long and 82.5 feet wide. South of Omro take County E for 0.3 mile east of State Highway 116. The prairie is on the north side of County E and unmarked. Park on the shoulder.

Lake Michigan

*. . . I walked the evenings away, year on year, except when mos-
quitoes plagued me too much or the cold became too intense.*
August Derleth, WALDEN WEST

1. Door County
2. Kewaunee County
3. Manitowoc County
4. Sheboygan County

Door County

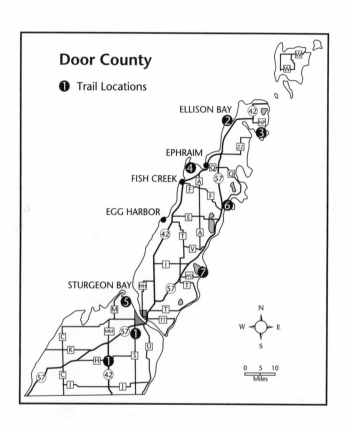

Door County

❶ Trail Locations

ELLISON BAY

EPHRAIM

FISH CREEK

EGG HARBOR

STURGEON BAY

N
W — E
S

0   5   10
Miles

1 Railroad Bed Trail Connects Door, Kewaunee Counties

Ahnapee State Trail, Sturgeon Bay–Algoma

The description of this trail occurs in the Kewaunee County section, pp. 90–93.

2 Park Has Scenic Overlook and Secluded Trails

Ellison Bluff County Park, west of Ellison Bay

State parks in Door County get crowded in summer. For a quiet place to do some hiking and perhaps enjoy a dramatic view of the sparkling waters of Green Bay while you're picnicking, try this secluded 88-acre county park.

Description and special features. Rustic footpaths start from the southern portion of the parking lot and wander through a woods of maple and old birch. A fork to the right from the main path goes dangerously across the face of the bluff, which is not fenced off. Avoid this route unless you're a very experienced hiker. Other paths are much safer.

Degree of difficulty. Except for the portion on the face of the bluff, paths are on mostly level terrain. They have a natural surface and are not maintained.

How to get there. About 1 mile southwest of downtown Ellison Bay on State Highway 42, go west on Porcupine Bay Road 1.2 miles to the parking lot.

Regulations. The park is open from 6:00 A.M. to 9:00 P.M. Camping is prohibited.

Facilities. A platform projects over the bluff to provide a startling view of Green Bay. There are also benches strategically placed to take advantage of the view. The park has parking for about 15 cars, pit toilets, and picnic tables.

Other points of interest in area

A second location with a little-known, secluded trail is *Meridian County Park and Lyle Harter-Matter Sanctuary*. The two properties total 122 acres. The trail, which is not maintained by the county, goes north for about 0.75 mile through the wooded sanctuary from a wayside park on the west side of State Highway 57. Located 2 miles north of Jacksonport, the wayside has toilets and picnic tables.

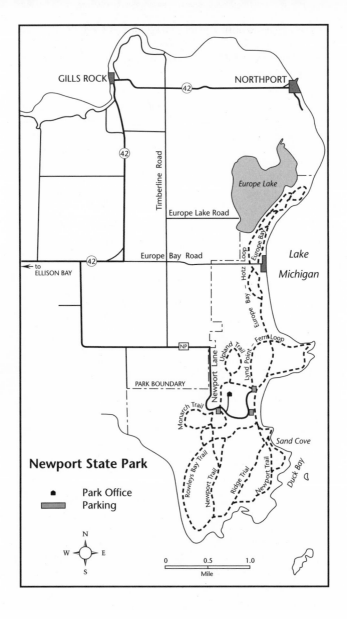

GILLS ROCK

NORTHPORT

42

Timberline Road

Europe Lake

Europe Lake Road

Europe Bay Road

42

to
ELLISON BAY

Loop

Holtz

Europe Bay

Europe Bay

Lake

Michigan

Ferm Loop

NP

Newport Lane

Upland Trail

Lynd Point

PARK BOUNDARY

Monarch Trail

Sand Cove

Rowleys Bay Trail

Newport Trail

Ridge Trail

Newport Trail

Duck Bay

Newport State Park

Park Office
Parking

N
W E
S

0   0.5   1.0
Mile

3 Pioneer Village History Haunts These Trails

Newport State Park, east of Ellison Bay

In the late nineteenth century pioneers cut a village out of the wilderness forest near the northern end of the Door Peninsula and called it Newport. They cut maple and bass cordwood, which fired Milwaukee brickyard kilns, and hemlock and cedar for railroad ties. Thinking soil that could grow such magnificent trees would also be fertile for crops, they attempted to farm the cleared land. But the rocky earth grew little wheat or crops for hay production.

Newport became a ghost town when the woodcutters departed for the northern pineries and the farmers took up more profitable endeavors elsewhere. As the land healed, it reverted to near-wilderness. In 1966, the state of Wisconsin purchased the property and, in 1977, established it as a wilderness park, with the goal of preserving its history and ecology through low-impact development. The park permits only backpack camping and has built just 1 mile of roads in 2,400 acres. However, more than 20 miles of hiking trails lace the restored wilderness and reveal its past.

Description and special features. Before hiking Newport, stop by the park office for two booklets. *Newport—Out of Wilderness Into Wilderness* provides historical information about locations on trails. *Forest Heritage Tour* guides the hiker on the Upland Trail, identifying both historical and ecological highlights. Newport has six trails. Assistant park manager Kirby Foss helped me with descriptions and difficulty ratings.

Europe Bay–Hotz Loop (5 miles) is the main trail going north into the isthmus between Europe Lake and Lake Michigan. South of Europe Bay Road it goes through deciduous forest, and north of the road through a mixture of trees including cedar, spruce, and hemlock. The Hotz Trail leads to the site of a log cottage built by the Hotz family, who bought and preserved the land after the loggers and farmers had gone. A water pump remains at the site.

Lynd Point–Fern Loop 👟 👟 👟 👟 (2.2 miles) goes along the Lake Michigan shore through many rock out-croppings. Near the north end of Lynd Point, a small path leads to the ruins of a pioneer cabin. The Fern Trail goes through a bog where lady slippers, marsh marigolds, trilliums, and he-patica blossom in their seasons.

Newport Trail and Sand Cove–Duck Bay Loop 👟 👟 👟 (5 miles) goes south from the parking lot through eastern boreal forest, which is a scientific area. The Duck Bay–Sand Cove portion follows the shoreline past Riley Point. The area was called Bohemia Town a century ago.

Rowleys Bay Trail 👟 👟 👟 👟 (4 miles) follows a rugged shoreline with rock outcroppings and goes through a pine plantation.

Upland Trail 👟 👟 (2 miles) is a self-guiding nature trail. Numbered posts are keyed to a printed guide, which is available at the park office. The tour includes an old root cellar, rock walls, and foundation ruins, as well as the identification of trees on the trail.

Monarch Trail 👟 👟 (1 mile) goes through a meadow. "I made this trail because I saw people looking out from the edge of the meadow. They were reluctant to venture into the tall grass," says assistant park manager Foss.

Degree of difficulty. While much of the terrain is level or gently sloping, some trails go over rocky outcroppings and rugged shoreline. Trails have natural surface and are, for the most part, wide and well maintained.

How to get there. From downtown Ellison Bay take State High-way 42 north and east 2.3 miles to County NP, then south and east 2.5 miles to South Newport Lane, then south 0.9 mile to the park.

Regulations. Day-use hours are 6:00 A.M. to 11:00 P.M. Dogs must be leashed. Picking or collecting of plants is prohibited, but you may pick edible fruits, nuts, and mushrooms. No motor vehicles are permitted. You may bicycle on several trails, as indicated by signs, and a separate bicycle trail map is available at the park office. Wear bright clothing during the firearm and late archery deer hunting seasons, since hunters also use the park. You may cross-country ski in season, but trails are not groomed. You'll need a state park annual or daily permit to bring your auto into the park.

Facilities. There are 16 backpack campsites distributed throughout the park, with pit toilets. All campsites are on park trails. The park also has a picnic area, two swimming beaches, and a bathhouse.

Other points of interest in area

North of the park at either Gills Rock or Northport, you can take a ferry to *Washington Island,* rent a bicycle at the dock, and tour this island that was settled by Scandinavians and Icelanders over 100 years ago. The ferry from Northport also accommodates autos. Take State Highway 42 north from its junction with County NP to either port.

Rock Island State Park offers the most secluded hiking in Door County. The 800-acre state park, reached by ferry from Washington Island, has 9.5 miles of marked hiking trails, many through thick forests. No wheeled vehicles are allowed. For those who wish to stay overnight, the park provides 40 rustic campsites. The state purchased the island from the estate of Chester H. Thordarson, an Iceland emigrant who lived there and built several structures, including an impressive stone boathouse that still stands. To reach Rock Island, take the Karfi ferry from Jackson Harbor.

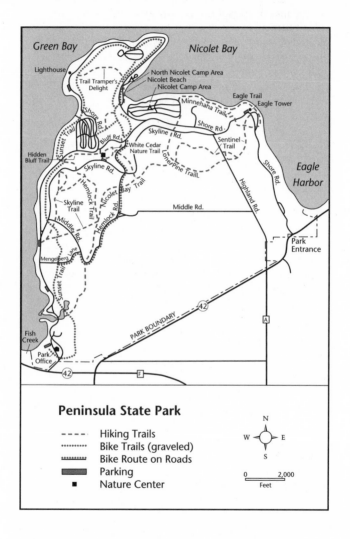

Green Bay

Nicolet Bay

Lighthouse

Trail Tramper's Delight

North Nicolet Camp Area
Nicolet Beach
Nicolet Camp Area

Minnehaha Trail

Eagle Trail
Eagle Tower

Shore Rd.

Shore Rd.

Sunset Trail

Skyline Rd.

Sentinel Trail

Bluff Rd.

White Cedar Nature Trail

Hidden Bluff Trail

Skyline Rd.

Lone Pine Trail

Eagle Harbor

Skyline Trail

Hemlock Trail

Nicolet Bay Trail

Middle Rd.

Hemlock Rd.

Highland Rd.

Shore Rd.

Middle Rd.

Mengelberg Lane

Sunset Trail

Park Entrance

Fish Creek

Park Office

PARK BOUNDARY

42

A

42

F

Peninsula State Park

- - - - Hiking Trails
.... Bike Trails (graveled)
▬▬▬ Bike Route on Roads
▨ Parking
■ Nature Center

N
W ◇ E
S

0   2,000
        Feet

4 Busy State Park Still Has Quiet Trails

Peninsula State Park, Fish Creek

Some hikers like quiet forests with secluded trails. Others like busy places with lots of people and a variety of things to do when they're not hiking. Surprisingly, this 3,763-acre park offers both. Although more than 1 million visitors enjoy the park each year, the trails are not heavily used, according to assistant superintendent Marcia Peeters.

Located on a choice wooded peninsula in a busy tourist area, the park is one of Wisconsin's most complete. When you're not hiking its well-maintained trails, you can play golf or tennis, take a lighthouse tour, or even attend the theater, all within the park. Of course, the park also provides camping, playgrounds, swimming, and nature programs—all the other activities you might expect at a full-service state park.

Description and special features. While I've visited the park many times, I haven't hiked all of its 20 miles of trails. I've used park-distributed literature as a major source for the following descriptions, and Ms. Peeters provided the difficulty ratings. Distances of trails given may include overlap with other trails.

White Cedar Nature Trail (0.5-mile loop) starts and ends near the Nature Center. Information stations tell about the life cycle of the white-tail deer and this animal's effects on the environment of the park. A fenced enclosure illustrates what conditions are like when no deer is present.

Sentinel Trail (2-mile loop) winds through stands of maple, beech, and red pine in a primitive area. Persons in wheelchairs may use a 0.6-mile graveled portion over gently rolling terrain. A printed guide available at the park office, and sometimes at the trailhead, identifies 21 trees and 14 flowers on the trail.

Sunset Trail 👟 (5.1 miles) also accommodates wheel-chairs on a graveled surface. Going through the entire west side of the park, users traverse every major type of landscape in the park. This is the only hiking trail also open to bicycles.

Hidden Bluff Trail 👟 (0.75 mile), a spur of the Sunset Trail, provides access to the Nature Center.

Nicolet Bay Trail 👟 👟 (2.2 miles) climbs through stands of upland hardwoods as well as cedar and hemlock. The trail connects with the Hemlock Trail (see below) and the Sentinel Trail. A spur goes to Nicolet Beach.

Hemlock Trail 👟 👟 👟 (1.8 miles) crosses the bluff line twice, going through quiet stands of hemlock and cedar. Atop the bluff the forest changes to such hardwoods as beech, maple, and birch. You may see the federally endangered dwarf lake iris on this trail.

Lone Pine Trail 👟 👟 👟 (0.6 mile) ascends the bluff that forms the backbone of the park and then winds through a hardwood forest. Hikers may return from the terminus via Sentinel or Nicolet Bay Trail.

Eagle Trail 👟 👟 👟 👟 👟 (2-mile loop), the most strenuous in the park, follows the water's edge and climbs the highest bluffs in Door County. Portions are steep and rocky. The trail parallels scenic Eagle Harbor for more than a mile.

Minnehaha Trail 👟 👟 (0.7 mile) goes along the Nicolet Bay shore, providing a connecting link between Eagle Trail and Nicolet Camp Area.

Trail Tramper's Delight 👟 👟 (0.6 mile) connects the lighthouse and the North Nicolet Camp Area. Its name is said to be derived from the cool walk its shaded route provides on a hot summer day.

Skyline Trail 👟 👟 (3-mile loop) climbs Sven's Bluff through hardwood forests and meadows on rolling terrain. Round-trip distance is via connecting trails.

Vita Course 👟 (1-mile loop) is an exercise course with 11 stations.

Degree of difficulty. Trails are generally wide, well-maintained, and have a natural surface except where indicated above. Terrain varies from flat or gently sloping in most areas of the park to very steep on the bluffs and some hills.

How to get there. The park's main entrance road goes north from State Highway 42 just east of Fish Creek.

Regulations. The park is open to day users from 6:00 A.M. to 11:00 P.M. Dogs, which are allowed on all trails except the White Cedar Nature Trail, must be leashed. No biking is permitted on hiking trails except the multiuse Sunset Trail. In a move that should be encouraged in other parks, Peninsula has separated hikers and mountain bikers by providing a separate mountain bike trail system. That trail is used by cross-country skiers in winter, and hikers are not allowed on it then either. However, the Sentinel and Minnehaha trails are kept open for hikers in winter. You'll need a state park annual or day pass on your auto to enter the park.

Facilities. A favorite among campers, Peninsula has four family campgrounds with a total of 469 sites. There are flush toilets, open until mid-October, and pit toilets. This well-equipped park also has swimming beaches with bathhouses, picnic grounds with shelters, boat launches, volleyball and tennis courts, an 18-hole golf course, an observation tower, a lighthouse, and a 650-seat outdoor amphitheater. You can rent bicycles, wind surfing equipment, canoes, and other water craft.

Other points of interest in area

The *village of Fish Creek* is within walking distance of the park office. This busy resort town has art galleries, restaurants, and shops galore. The Old Peninsula Festival, in July, is a favorite with parades, a carnival, and fireworks. A music festival is also held. Phone the Visitor Information Center at 414-868-2316.

5 Hiking Trails Feature Ledge and Glacial Geology

Potawatomi State Park, Sturgeon Bay

Sitting atop the Niagara Escarpment, a limestone ledge that forms the spine of Door County, Potawatomi State Park juts out into Sturgeon Bay. From its forested trails, hikers can enjoy sweeping views of the bay and geological features formed by the continental glacier and subsequent widely varying lake levels. Wildlife includes deer, porcupines, foxes, and 50 species of nesting birds.

Description and special features. Two hiking trails and a nature trail will take you throughout the park. Assistant park superintendent Kent Harrison provided difficulty ratings.

Hemlock Trail (2.5 miles) circles the southeast half of the park. Starting at the Sturgeon Bay shoreline, it goes into the interior of the park through mixed pine and hardwood forest. A portion of the trail traces the 8,500-year-old shoreline of postglacial Lake Algonquin.

Tower Trail (3.5 miles) loops through the northwest half of the park. From the trailhead at the top of the downhill ski area you can see the waters of Green Bay and the rolling terrain of Door County. Then hikers proceed along the highest bluff in the park and reach a 75-foot observation tower, which affords an even better view. The trail descends the bluff to the shoreline and goes through a cedar woods before returning to the top.

Portions of the above trails, starting at the observation tower and exiting the park at Duluth Avenue, have been designated as a segment of the Ice Age National Scenic Trail.

Ancient Shores Nature Trail (0.5 mile). From this short looping path you can see the remains of two postglacial lake shorelines. The trail begins at Norway Road. Obtain a

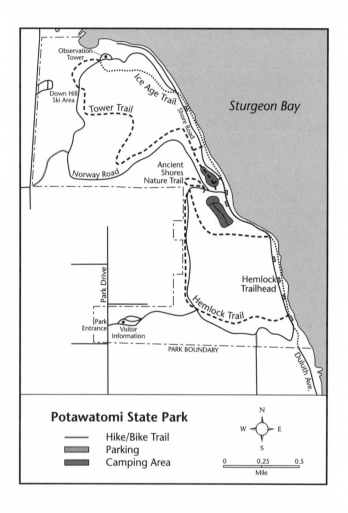

Observation
Tower

Down Hill
Ski Area

Ice Age Trail

Tower Trail

Shore Road

Sturgeon Bay

Norway Road

Ancient
Shores
Nature Trail

Park Drive

Hemlock
Trailhead

Hemlock Trail

Park
Entrance

Visitor
Information

PARK BOUNDARY

Duluth Ave.

Potawatomi State Park

——— Hike/Bike Trail

▨ Parking

▰ Camping Area

N
W ✦ E
S

0   0.25   0.5
Mile

printed guide, keyed to 14 information stations, at Visitor Information to learn about the old landforms and other trail highlights.

Degree of difficulty. Portions of the Tower and Hemlock trails follow the lakeside bluffs, where footing is sometimes tenuous and slopes are steep. Inclines elsewhere, and on the Ancient Shores Nature Trail, are more gentle. Surfacing varies from asphalt on a portion of the Hemlock Trail to bare natural surface on most of the other hiking trails. A separate bicycle trail shares the path with a short segment of the Hemlock Trail.

How to get there. From State Highways 57 and 42 just southwest of the city of Sturgeon Bay, take Park Drive north 2.4 miles to the park entrance on the right.

Regulations. For day users, park hours are 6:00 A.M. to 11:00 P.M. A state park annual or daily permit is required. Pets must be leashed and are not allowed on the Ancient Shores Nature Trail. Bikes are not permitted on hiking trails except on a short portion of the Hemlock Trail where signs indicate. Both cross-country skiing and snowmobiling are allowed. Obtain a winter trail map at Visitor Information.

Facilities. This full-service park provides facilities for camping, swimming, and picnicking. Phone 414-746-2890. There are restrooms and drinking water near the Hemlock trailhead and at the observation tower on the Tower Trail.

Other points of interest in area

In the city of Sturgeon Bay, adults and children enjoy the *Door County Historical Museum.* In the Pioneer Fire Company wing, children can climb into the driver's seat of a restored 1924 fire truck and ring its bell. On another level visit an old-time doctor's office, music shop, jewelry store, barber shop, and grocery store.

The museum is at Fourth and Michigan streets. Hours are 10:00 A.M. to 5:00 P.M. May 1 through November 1. There is a small admission fee.

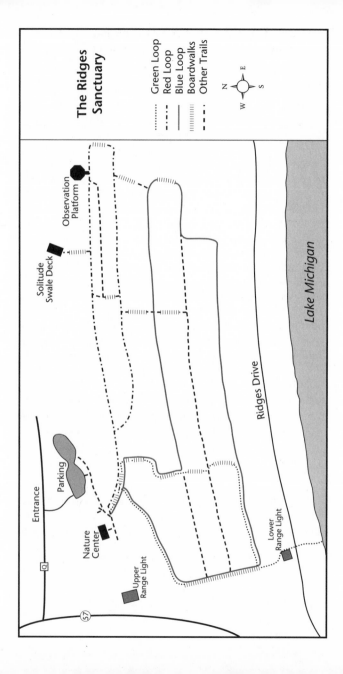

The Ridges Sanctuary

········· Green Loop
—··—·· Red Loop
——— Blue Loop
ııııııııı Boardwalks
— —— Other Trails

Observation Platform

Solitude Swale Deck

Entrance

Parking

Nature Center

Upper Range Light

Lower Range Light

Ridges Drive

Lake Michigan

57

6 Nature Sanctuary Reveals Lakeside History, Ecology

The Ridges Sanctuary, Baileys Harbor

Over two sets of cycles, one 30 years long and the other about 150 years, Lake Michigan's water level rises and falls. With each cycle in places like the Ridges Sanctuary, a beach ridge is formed. Recent core soil samples reveal there are about 30 such ridges there, some overlapping others. Seventeen are very prominent.

Rare plants abound in the sanctuary's boreal forest. Some 25 species of orchid grow there. The staff recently learned the sanctuary probably harbors the nation's largest population of a federally endangered insect, Hine's emerald dragonfly.

Established in 1937, Ridges became Wisconsin's first designated natural area in 1967. It is also listed as a national natural landmark.

Description and special features. Trail planners divided the Ridges' 3.4 miles of walking trails into three loops to provide walks of various lengths. Along the trails, 39 numbered posts key to a printed guide available for a small donation at the Nature Center.

The parallel trails follow the tops of the ridges through a forest of northern white cedar, white spruce, balsam fir, and white pine. Frequent boardwalks across intervening swales connect the trails. A long boardwalk on the blue and green trails runs between two tower-mounted range lights used by early navigators to find a safe channel into Baileys Harbor.

Degree of difficulty. Trails are mostly level, wide, and have a natural or wood-chip surface. Well-constructed boardwalks cross wetlands. The Ridges sanctuary is designed for leisurely strolling among its many natural features.

How to get there. From State Highway 57 on the north side of Baileys Harbor, take County Q northeast 0.1 mile to the sanctuary's entrance on the right.

Regulations. The sanctuary prohibits the following: pets, wheeled vehicles of any kind, collecting or removal of plants, straying from trails, picnicking, smoking, and littering. Since the Ridges is supported entirely by private funds, it requests a donation from visitors. The Nature Center is open 9:00 A.M. to 4:00 P.M. Monday through Saturday, and 1:00 P.M. to 4:00 P.M. Sunday, from mid-May to mid-October, with the exception of major holiday closings. You may join guided tours Monday through Saturday at 9:30 A.M. and 1:30 P.M. from June through August. You may cross-country ski, but trails are not groomed. Restrooms are closed in winter.

Facilities. The Nature Center has a small retail shop. Restrooms are in a separate building. A reconstructed log cabin, used for programs and meetings, was moved to the sanctuary.

Other points of interest in area

Tofte Point Natural Area provides a more rustic hiking experience. Unmaintained footpaths take the hiker to a rocky shoreline and a former lighthouse location. The area was deeded by The Nature Conservancy to the University of Wisconsin–Green Bay. From State Highway 57 in Baileys Harbor, go 2.5 miles on Ridges Drive. A gravel road from the point will take you an additional mile out onto the peninsula. At the end is an unmarked, little-used, hard-to-follow footpath on which it would be easy to get lost.

7 Walk with the Spirits of Ancient Inhabitants among Lakeside Dunes

Whitefish Dunes State Park, south of Jacksonport

The state established this park in 1967 to protect some of the largest sand dunes in Wisconsin, including "Old Baldy," which is 93 feet high. The newest dunes of loose sand supporting thin vegetation border the Lake Michigan beach. Farther from the lake in the forest, successively older "stabilized" dunes form tiers behind the most recently formed dunes.

For millennia, access to excellent fishing has attracted people to the site. Archaeologists have discovered at least eight stages of occupation in the park, ranging back more than 2,000 years. A variety of park-built trails enables hikers to experience the uniqueness of this place.

The park naturalist conducts group nature hikes, especially during the summer. Check at the park office for a schedule.

Description and special features. Five major trails and several spurs wander for 13 miles, including overlapping, through the 900-acre park. For the following descriptions of trails—especially those portions I did not have an opportunity to walk—I depended heavily upon literature provided by the park. Park superintendent Allen Miller provided difficulty ratings.

Red Trail 👟 👟 (2.8 miles) takes the hiker on two successive loops behind the newest dunes to Old Baldy, the park's highest dune. A platform atop the dune provides an overlook of Lake Michigan and Clark Lake, which borders the park on the north.

Green Trail 👟 👟 (1.8 miles). After following the base of a stabilized dune, heavily forested with hemlocks and white pines, the trail loops back through a beech and maple woods. A 0.7-mile spur goes to Clark Lake.

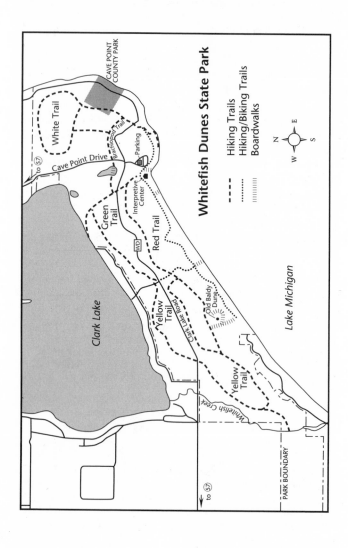

Whitefish Dunes State Park

CAVE POINT COUNTY PARK

White Trail

Brachiopod Trail

Parking

to 57

Cave Point Drive

Green Trail

Interpretive Center

Red Trail

WD

Yellow Trail

Old Baldy Dune

Clark Lake Road

Clark Lake

Yellow Trail

Whitefish Creek

Lake Michigan

to 57

PARK BOUNDARY

N
E
W
S

Hiking Trails
Hiking/Biking Trails
Boardwalks

Yellow Trail 👟 👟 (4.2 miles). Forming a loop and branching off the Green Trail, this trail goes through dry, sandy terrain and a plantation of red pines. A 0.1-mile spur extends to Whitefish Creek.

White Trail 👟 👟 (2.5 miles). A double loop goes through a forest of mixed hardwoods. Cave Point County Park (see below) can be reached via a connecting trail.

Brachiopod Trail 👟 (1.5 miles). An informative booklet available at the park office explains the numbered stations on this interpretive trail. The guide talks about the flora, fauna, geology, and archaeology of the park. A brachiopod, the guide explains, was a one-footed clamlike creature whose fossils remain in the rock from many millions of years ago. This trail is wheelchair accessible.

Degree of difficulty. Trails are wide and well maintained on terrain with only mild slopes. They have mostly natural surface, with those nearest the beach being sandy. Some rocks are exposed in the shallow soil of the White Trail. Compacted limestone screenings pave the Brachiopod Trail and a railed boardwalk crosses a wetland.

How to get there. From State 57 in Jacksonport, take Cave Point Drive 3.1 miles south to the park's gate. From State Highway 57 just north of Valmy and west of the park, take County WD (Clark Lake Road) east 3.8 miles.

Regulations. Open hours are 8:00 A.M. to 8:00 P.M. daily. Pets are allowed on a leash except in picnic areas and buildings and on groomed ski trails. To prevent erosion, walking and climbing are not allowed on the beachside dunes except where steps have been provided. Mountain bikes are prohibited except on portions of the red and white trails where signs indicate. No motor vehicles are allowed. Trails are groomed for cross-country skiing in winter, except the White Trail, which is reserved for hiking, snow shoeing, and leashed pets.

Facilities. This day-use park has a visitors' interpretive center, open daily the year around from 8:00 A.M. to 4:30 P.M. Flush toilets and drinking water are available there, and there are pit toilets elsewhere in the park. Other facilities include a picnic shelter and grills, a swimming beach, and a bathhouse. (However, the swimming beach was closed in 1997 because of high lake levels.)

Other points of interest in area

Cave Point County Park, a park within Whitefish Dunes State Park, can be reached by foot via a connector to the White Trail, or by road from a separate entrance just north of the state park entrance. Lake Michigan waves that have pounded ledges of Niagara limestone for an untold number of years formed shoreline caves. A hollow drumlike sound emits from the caves when the waves lap into them. This park has pit toilets, parking, and picnic tables.

Kewaunee County

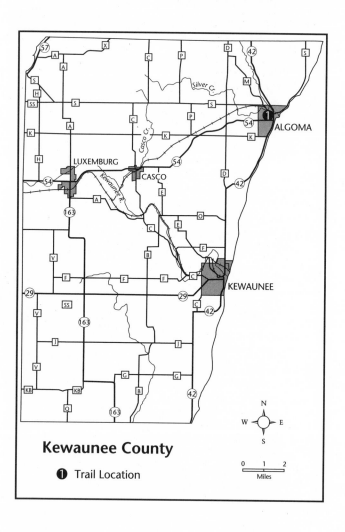

Kewaunee County

1 Trail Location

0   1   2
Miles

1 Railroad Bed Trail Connects Door, Kewaunee Counties

Ahnapee State Trail, Sturgeon Bay–Algoma

Following an abandoned railroad bed in a giant arc, this 15-mile multipurpose trail is open to hiking, biking, horseback riding, and snowmobiling. With trailheads just south of Sturgeon Bay and in downtown Algoma, the trail will take you through quiet villages, rolling farmlands, and along the Ahnapee River. It's been certified as part of the Ice Age National Scenic Trail.

Description and special features. At this writing Sturgeon Bay authorities plan to extend the trail into the city. From its present trailhead, it goes southwest for 10.5 miles through Maplewood and curves southeast through Forestville to County X at the Door-Kewaunee County line. A favorite, picturesque 5-mile portion of the trail is from Forestville to Algoma along the Ahnapee River. It goes through the Ahnapee Wildlife Area and hardwood forests with many wildflowers.

Degree of difficulty. A paving of crushed limestone provides a solid base for all uses. As a former railroad bed, the trail has almost zero grade. Regular improvements, including the recent replacement of a bridge in Kewaunee County, have made the trail easy to walk.

How to get there. From State Highways 42 and 57 just south of Sturgeon Bay, take Shiloh Road south 1 mile to Leewards Street, then west and south 0.5 mile to a parking lot at the end of a gravel road on the left. At this writing, construction underway in downtown Algoma extends the trail to a trailhead just west of the corner of Fourth and Navarino streets.

Regulations. Hiking, biking, horseback riding, and snowmobiling are allowed. Dogs must be leashed.

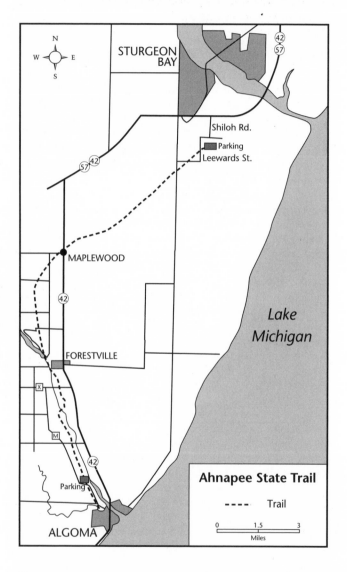

Facilities. There are restrooms at the north trailhead parking lot. In Forestville the trail goes through the 79-acre Forestville Dam Park, which has restrooms and a picnic area. Parking and restrooms are provided at the Algoma trailhead.

Other points of interest in area

The *Maritime Museum* in Sturgeon Bay reflects the city's history as one of the Great Lakes' leading shipbuilding and boating communities. In the former offices of the Roen Steamship Company, see a refurbished pilothouse and examples of restored early twentieth-century craft. Displays show how ships are built. Located at the foot of Florida Street next to Sunset Park, the museum is open 10:00 A.M. to 4:00 P.M. daily from Memorial Day to mid-October.

Manitowoc County

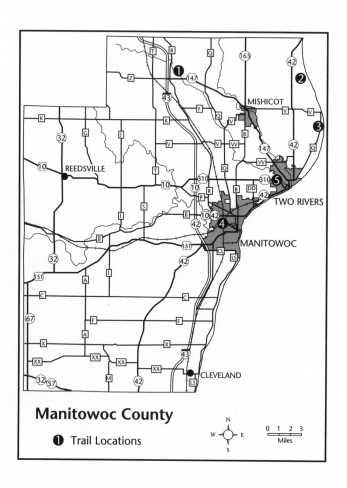

Manitowoc County

1 Trail Locations

N
W — E
S

0 1 2 3
Miles

1 Hike in a Rain Forest in Wisconsin?

Cherney Maribel Caves County Park, Maribel

It had rained the night before I walked the trails at Maribel Caves. To get to this deep valley of the West Twin River, I descended a winding entrance road to the parking lot, walked down a path, and took several flights of wooden stairs to the trails below the cliff line.

Within minutes the environment changed from sunny rural fields of the park entrance above to perpetually moist, deeply shaded, old-growth cedar and hemlock forest in the river valley. The humid stillness, the dripping branches, the cedars' buttressing surface roots across the path took me back in memory to my trek through a Costa Rican rain forest the previous winter.

I'm sure on another day—say, in January—my impression would have been different. But on the warm June day of my walk, I was as close to a rain forest as I could get in Wisconsin.

Description and special features. The trails run northeast and southwest between the river and a sheer cliff line. The cliff, believed to be eroded into the Niagara dolomite bedrock by the continental glacier, contains several caves you can see from the paths. A number of springs seep from the limestone and flow over moss-covered rocks toward the river. The moist soil produces a rich variety of ferns, wildflowers, and creeping plants among the standing and fallen ancient conifers that dominate the forest.

Additional trails in the upper park follow the cliff line through mostly northern hardwoods.

The natural beauty of the park had attracted visitors long before it was acquired by the county in 1963. A wishing well was built around one spring in the northern part of the park. North of the park an old monastery was later turned into a hotel.

Degree of difficulty. While most of the paths below the cliff line are level and easy to walk, surface roots or bare bedrock cover some portions. Trails are occasionally narrow and steep and can be slippery. During my morning visit after an evening rain, there were a few standing puddles and muddy spots. The park has built wooden boardwalks over several permanently moist areas. From the parking lot, a gravel-paved entrance path leads to wooden stairs that descend the cliff.

How to get there. From I-43 near Maribel take State Highway 147 east 0.3 mile to County R, and north 0.5 mile to the park entrance on the right.

Regulations. The park is open from 6:00 A.M. to 10:00 P.M. Pets must be leashed. Trail bikes are discouraged. The park is not officially open in winter for cross-country skiing.

Facilities. The upper part of the 75-acre park has parking, pit toilets, a picnic shelter, a water pump, and a recreation area with playground equipment.

Other points of interest in area

You can hike the kettle moraine in *Walla Hi County Park* 4 miles east of Kiel in southwestern Manitowoc County. This 160-acre park has picnic areas, playground equipment, toilet facilities, a spring-fed pond, and an abandoned fish hatchery.

2 Learn about Energy's Role in Nature on This Trail

Point Beach Energy Center Nature Trail

At Point Beach Energy Center, not only can you walk a nature trail; you can also experience the exhibits at the visitors' center of this working nuclear electric-generating plant. The exhibits let you generate your own electricity, step inside a model nuclear reactor, and play computer games.

Description and special features. The 0.6-mile nature trail, through a climax forest located near the visitors' center, is divided into two sections. Allow about 20 minutes for the "short circuit" and 40 minutes for the whole trail. Information stations along the way emphasize the interdependence of plants, animals, and energy. A rotating wheel with pointers on the longer trail helps with the identification of trees in the forest. You'll also see trilliums, jack-in-the-pulpits, and bloodroot during their seasons.

Degree of difficulty. This very well maintained trail is paved with wood chips for its entire length. Gently rolling dune terrain provides a leisurely walking experience.

How to get there. From 2 miles north of Mishicot on State Highway 163, take Nuclear Road east to signs showing the property's entrance on the left. From Two Rivers take State Highway 42 north 7 miles to Nuclear Road, then east to the entrance.

Regulations. The visitors' center is open the year around except December 24, 25, 31, January 1, Easter, and Thanksgiving. Hours are 9:00 A.M. to 4:30 P.M. daily during April through October; 10:00 A.M. to 4:30 P.M. Monday–Friday, and 12:00 noon to 4:30 P.M. Saturday and Sunday, during November through March. Fishing is allowed off the Point Beach plant pier.

Facilities. Parking and restrooms are available. There is an observation tower on top of the visitors' center.

Other points of interest in area

In 1881 Ed Berners invented the ice cream sundae in Two Rivers, 7 miles south of Point Beach Energy Center. The *Historic Washington House Museum,* 1622 Jefferson Street, has a working replica of his ice cream parlor, where you can enjoy a sundae, a cherry coke, or root beer made "from scratch." Also visit the *Historical Society's Convent Museum* at 1810 Jefferson. Call 414-793-2490 for information.

3 These Trails Are on Ancient Sand Dunes

Point Beach State Forest, north of Two Rivers

Look out from the shore of Lake Michigan, and it seems the waves from that huge inland sea have forever washed up to where you stand. Not so. In the 12,000 years since the Laurentide Ice Sheet receded northward, lake levels have fluctuated hundreds of feet. For example, postglacial Lake Algonquin, a Great Lakes predecessor, covered many square miles of land now dry near the existing lake.

That lake and others since then receded in stages. With each new water level, a new shoreline was established. On the shore, windblown sand formed rows of dunes. At places like Point Beach State Forest, the dunes gradually became a forest when the lake receded and left them farther from shore. In between the dunes, swales often retained water to become marshes. This is how the "ridges and swales" terrain of this state forest came about.

Description and special features. Two main trails and a small nature trail run through the 2,900-acre forest. The trails follow the tops of ridges and go from one ridge to another. Hemlocks, red and white pines, maples, beeches, birches, and oaks predominate in this tension zone forest. With the many marshes, small snakes and frogs frequently cross the trails, and mosquitoes invite hikers to a grand feast.

The Ridges Trail. The first of three connecting loops begins at the Nature Center parking lot. The red loop is 3 miles; the blue and red loops combined, 5.5 miles. Add the yellow loop for a total trail length of 7.25 miles.

The Red Pine Trail. Accessed at either of two parking lots west of County O, a single loop and hilly middle trail total 3.1 miles.

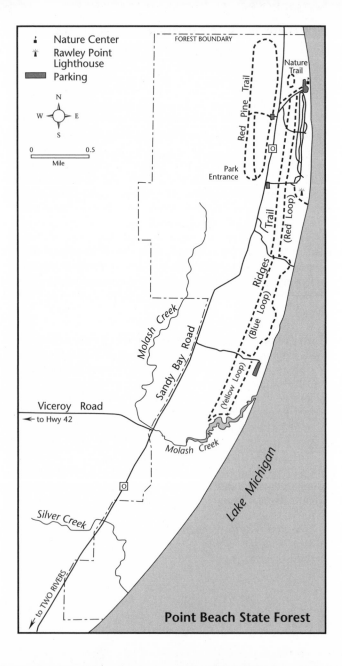

Nature Center
Rawley Point Lighthouse
Parking

FOREST BOUNDARY

Nature Trail

Red Pine Trail

Park Entrance

Trail

Ridges

(Red Loop)

(Blue Loop)

(Yellow Loop)

Molash Creek

Sandy Bay Road

Viceroy Road
← to Hwy 42

Molash Creek

Silver Creek

to TWO RIVERS

Lake Michigan

N
W E
S

0   0.5
Mile

Point Beach State Forest

Nature Trail. Being rerouted at this writing, it will still begin north of the Nature Center and go about 0.75 mile.

Degree of difficulty. Most trails are wide with a natural surface. The variable terrain of the ridges makes some slopes steep. Trails are generally well maintained. Bring mosquito repellent.

How to get there. The forest is 4.5 miles north of Two Rivers on County O.

Regulations. Open 6:00 A.M. to 11:00 P.M. for day users. Dogs must be leashed on trails except when being used for hunting. Mountain bikes are permitted only on the Red Pine Trail. A state park annual or daily permit is required.

Facilities. The forest is nearly as fully equipped as a state park, with bathrooms, picnic facilities, camping, and concession stand. With its Lake Michigan location, it has a 6-mile sandy beach shoreline for water sports or walking.

Other points of interest in area

Rawley Point Lighthouse was built on the point in 1894. The light is located atop a steel tower 113 feet above the lake's surface and can be seen from up to 19 miles. Before the lighthouse was built, 26 ships foundered or were stranded on the point, including a large steamer that took 36 crewmen and passengers down with her. The lighthouse is closed to visitors, and no tours are available.

4 City Park Trail Offers Fitness Stations

Henry R. Schuette Park, Manitowoc

In the city of Manitowoc, you can walk a trail along the river, around a prairie, and through the woods. Or you can jog it and exercise at 18 fitness stations.

Description and special features. At the park's location, the Manitowoc River meanders through a deep valley with high banks. The 67.5-acre park occupies land both in the valley and atop the bank. From a parking lot in the lower park, a trail paved with limestone screenings follows the river to a prairie of several acres. You can follow a loop around the prairie and return to the trailhead, or you can take a longer route via an adjoining loop through a riverside woods.

If you're into knee bends, push ups, beam walking, and so on, you can do your thing at 18 "Exer-Trail" stations on the prairie and woods loops of the trail.

Degree of difficulty. Approximately 1.5 miles, the trail goes over mostly flat terrain with a few short inclines. A boardwalk bridges some lowland along the river. A portion of the trail, along the river, is paved with limestone screenings.

How to get there. The main parking lot for the lower park is off Broadway Street just east of the river. You can also reach the trail from a lot at the end of Clay Pit Road. Parking for the upper park is east of Broadway Street at Meadow Lane. Stairs descend the steep bank between the upper and lower portions of the park.

Regulations. The park is open from 6:00 A.M. to 11:00 P.M. No dogs or cats are allowed. Trails are groomed for cross-country skiing.

Facilities. Restrooms, benches, and a children's playground are in the upper park.

Other points of interest in area

On *the waterfront in Manitowoc,* you can walk or bike a paved 1.75-mile path and tour the *U.S.S. Cobia,* a submarine that was built during World War II in the city's shipbuilding works. The Wisconsin Maritime Museum, the Manitowoc Marina, a YMCA, a hotel, and a lakeside park are also along the way.

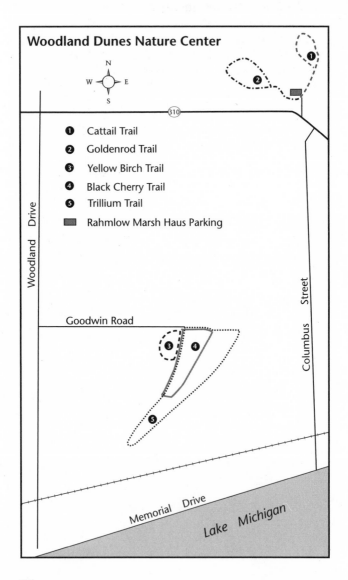

Woodland Dunes Nature Center

N
W · E
S

310

- ❶ Cattail Trail
- ❷ Goldenrod Trail
- ❸ Yellow Birch Trail
- ❹ Black Cherry Trail
- ❺ Trillium Trail
- ▩ Rahmlow Marsh Haus Parking

Woodland Drive

Columbus Street

Goodwin Road

❸ ❹

❺

Memorial Drive

Lake Michigan

5 Walk Boardwalks or Rustic Trails in Nature Preserve

Woodland Dunes Nature Center, between Manitowoc and Two Rivers

An oasis of marshland, swamps, sandy meadows, and wooded ridges, this privately supported preserve has five trails and a variety of activities for nature lovers.

Description and special features. These trails, situated in two separate areas, let you experience the safety and convenience of a boardwalk or the adventure of back-country hiking. Two of the trails start near the Rahmlow Marsh Haus, which serves as a nature center and office.

Cattail Trail goes on a boardwalk for 0.25 mile through a cattail marsh and swamp. It is wheelchair accessible.

Goldenrod Trail goes for 0.75 mile through a restored native prairie around Todd's Pond.

The other three trails begin in a separate wilderness area off Goodwin Road.

Yellow Birch Trail, a 0.25-mile boardwalk, was built so that people in wheelchairs could experience a trail through a swamp, according to center director Bernie Brouchoud.

Black Cherry Trail, 0.75 mile, follows ridges that used to be sand dunes when Lake Michigan's shoreline was far to the west of its present position. Wooden bridges cross swales in between the ridges.

Trillium Trail traverses terrain similar to that of the Black Cherry Trail but is about twice as long. Printed nature guides help with the identification of plants, birds, and wildlife on the Cattail, Goldenrod, and Yellow Birch trails.

Degree of difficulty. Difficulty ranges from easy on board-walks to more challenging on the narrow paths through the ridge and swale terrain of the wilderness area. The latter paths can be muddy in wet weather, but slopes are generally mild.

How to get there. The Rahmlow Marsh Haus, a brick farm-house over 100 years old, which serves as a temporary nature center and office, is at the intersection of State Highway 310 and Columbus Street on the western edge of Two Rivers. To reach the trails in the wilderness area between Two Rivers and Mani-towoc, from State Highway 310 take Woodland Drive south 1 mile to Goodwin Road, then east to the end of the road. The trailhead is on the right.

Regulations. Trails are open day and night the year around. Boardwalks permit hiking during the winter, when the other trails are used by cross-country skiers, Brouchoud informs us. No bikes or pets are allowed.

Supported privately, Woodland Dunes would welcome your donations. Send them to P.O. Box 2108, Manitowoc, WI 54221-2108.

Facilities. Parking is available, and there are restrooms in the Rahmlow Marsh Haus. Open hours are not posted, since the Marsh Haus must be closed when the staff member is called away.

Other points of interest in area

The *Rahmlow Marsh Haus* centers on a variety of activities in the preserve including bird banding, nature programs and slide shows for school classes, research projects, plant and wildlife identification projects, and the publication of a quarterly news-letter for members.

Sheboygan County

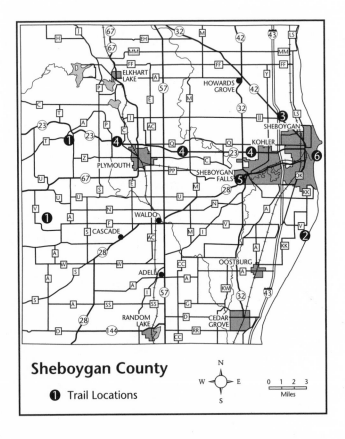

Sheboygan County

❶ Trail Locations

N
W — E
S

0 1 2 3
Miles

1 Trails Reveal State's Glacial Past

Northern Unit, Kettle Moraine State Forest

If you have an interest in Wisconsin's glacial history, you'll feel a certain excitement when hiking the trails of the Kettle Moraine State Forest. The Northern Unit, which occupies about 27,670 acres in three counties, displays its many classic glacial landforms with the casual aplomb of Zsa Zsa Gabor showing off her diamonds.

Kettles and kames are on every side. The moraines, formed by two lobes of the Laurentide Ice Sheet when they melted more than 10 centuries ago, seem larger here than anywhere else in the state. The Parnell Esker, a miles-long ridge of sand and gravel deposited by a glacier-born stream, towers 35-feet high in places.

Add to this the forest's 50-some species of trees and abundant wildlife for a first-class hiking experience.

Description and special features.

Hiking Trails

Glacial Trail. 🥾 🥾 🥾 🥾 This 31-mile trail, a segment of the Ice Age National Scenic Trail, is the longest, and accordingly the most rigorous, of the Kettle Moraine State Forest. It begins in the southwest at County H and goes north toward New Fane. It continues north to the Mauthe Lake Recreation Area, passes Crooked Lake, and generally trends northeast to join the Butler Lake Trail on the Parnell Esker. Continuing northeast, it briefly joins a portion of the Parnell Tower Trail, and then heads toward the Greenbush Kettle, a classic water-filled depression near the Greenbush Recreational Area. It then heads toward its northeast trailhead at County P near Glenbeulah, with a spur going northwest to Greenbush.

New Fane Trails. 🥾 🥾 Four trails, totaling 7.7 miles, were designed primarily for cross-country skiing. They curve

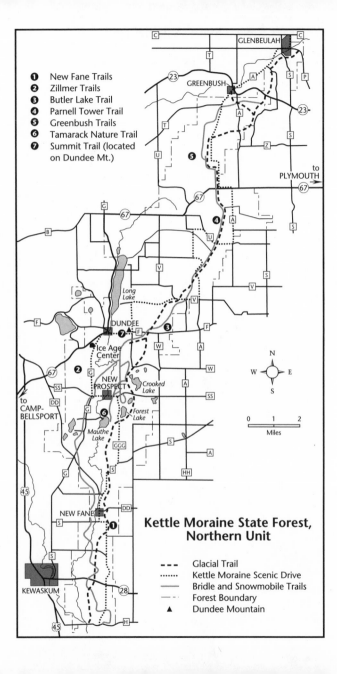

❶ New Fane Trails
❷ Zillmer Trails
❸ Butler Lake Trail
❹ Parnell Tower Trail
❺ Greenbush Trails
❻ Tamarack Nature Trail
❼ Summit Trail (located on Dundee Mt.)

GLENBEULAH

GREENBUSH

to PLYMOUTH

DUNDEE

Long Lake

Ice Age Center

NEW PROSPECT

Crooked Lake

Forest Lake

Mauthe Lake

to CAMP-BELLSPORT

NEW FANE

KEWASKUM

N
W ○ E
S

0   1   2
Miles

Kettle Moraine State Forest, Northern Unit

- - - Glacial Trail
.... Kettle Moraine Scenic Drive
Bridle and Snowmobile Trails
Forest Boundary
▲ Dundee Mountain

gently on wide paths. Again, these trails go through both hard-wood forest and a pine plantation, the latter more extensive. There is a picnic area at the trailhead.

Zillmer Trails. A network of four trails totals 11.4 miles. Typical hummocky moraine topography surrounds a small stream meandering through the area. Common forest hardwoods are oak, sugar maple, and basswood. On the yellow trail is a scenic overlook of a glacial outwash plain. Picnic tables, water, and toilets are available at the trailhead.

Butler Lake Trail. About the last fifth of this 3.1-mile trail goes atop the Parnell Esker, the most prominent esker in the Kettle Moraine State Forest. Initially the trail parallels the Parnell Esker, then it climbs to the top of the esker for a short distance. Leaving the esker, it proceeds through the forest and along small glacial marshes. It then loops back to its beginning atop the esker. You'll get an excellent view of Butler Lake from the top of the esker at the trail's end. Many birches and hickory trees grow near the trail.

Parnell Tower Trail. This rigorous 3.5-mile trail goes by means of stairs from the trailhead parking lot directly to an esker-top tower. You'll encounter steep slopes over the Green Bay Moraine as you hike through a hardwood forest. The northernmost portion briefly follows a power line maintenance road. The trail then turns south through a pine plantation and marshy lowlands. It joins the Glacial Trail at shelter #4. Enjoy a scenic overview there of kames and an outwash plain. The trail then loops back to the tower.

Greenbush Trails. The largest parking lot is north of the trailhead. The parklike trailhead has restrooms and a picnic area. A network of four trails totals 11 miles. As the first trails developed in the Kettle Moraine State Forest, some of them follow old logging roads. Hardwoods make up most of the forest here, but some portions of the yellow trail go through pine plantations. Toward the southern point of the yellow trail, enjoy an excellent scenic overview of Bear Lake. Though these trails were once a favorite of wildlife watchers, recent access given to mountain bikes has changed the trails' quiet nature, says naturalist Rodger Reif.

Nature Trails

Tamarack Nature Trail. Near the forest headquarters, this short trail goes around Mauthe Lake. Lowland hardwoods —alder, black ash, willow, tamarack, and cedar—are common. It traverses the Mauthe Lake Recreation Area for about a third of the trail's length. The trail will be moist during wet seasons. At this writing, forest supervisors plan to reconstruct informational stations on the trail and write an accompanying brochure.

Summit Trail. "This is the trail I'd recommend for someone who wants a great hiking experience, but can spend only a short time in the forest," says naturalist Reif. It crosses the crest of the forest's highest kame, Dundee Mountain. The trail is accessible from the south at a gate off County F. Park in a lot across the road about 100 feet west of the gate. Access from the north begins in the F Area Campground.

A dirt road, closed to vehicles, leads to the trailhead, which starts on steps going east toward the kame. Benches between flights of stairs afford a dramatic view of the surrounding landscape, including Long Lake to the northwest. From the 270-foot summit, you can see Lake Michigan 23 miles to the east on a clear day, says Reif. The trail loops back to the dirt road.

Two additional brief nature trails are the ***Moraine Ridge Nature Trail,*** near the Ice Age Visitor Center, and the ***Chip 'n' Chatter Nature Trail,*** near the Indoor Group Camp.

Degree of difficulty. The hummocky up-and-down terrain, typical of glacial lateral and terminal moraines, provides strenuous walking exercise. The Glacial Trail, which was designed as a back-country footpath, is narrow with many turns. Zillmer, Greenbush, and New Fane forest trails, used for cross-country skiing and biking as well as hiking, are wider and tend to have fewer sharp curves. Nearly all trails have natural surfaces, including naturally occurring glacial gravel. Skiing trails are groomed in winter and are not open to hikers when snow covered.

How to get there. Go northeast from Campbellsport on State Highway 67, or east from Kewaskum on State Highway 28, or west from Plymouth on State Highway 23. All trails and recreational facilities are either located or signed along the Kettle Moraine Scenic Drive, which runs through the entire forest.

Regulations. Open hours are: forest to noncampers—6:00 A.M. to 11:00 P.M.; forest headquarters—7:45 A.M. to 4:30 P.M. Monday through Friday; Ice Age Center—8:30 A.M. to 4:00 P.M. Monday through Friday, and 9:30 A.M. to 5:00 P.M. Saturday and Sunday. Dogs must be leashed and are not allowed on nature trails. Trail bikes are allowed only on the Greenbush, New Fane, and Zillmer trails. You'll need a state park annual or daily permit for your auto.

Facilities. The Kettle Moraine State Forest has nearly all the facilities of a well-developed state park: camping, swimming beaches, restrooms, and equestrian trails. There is ample parking at major trails. Backpackers may use any of five rustic shelters along the Glacial Trail or one on the Zillmer Trail.

Other points of interest in area

In the Kettle Moraine State Forest, you may watch an excellent interpretive film and collect information at the *Henry S. Reuss Ice Age Visitor Center,* located 0.5 mile south of Dundee on State Highway 67. The forest naturalist offers programs at the center from late spring through early fall.

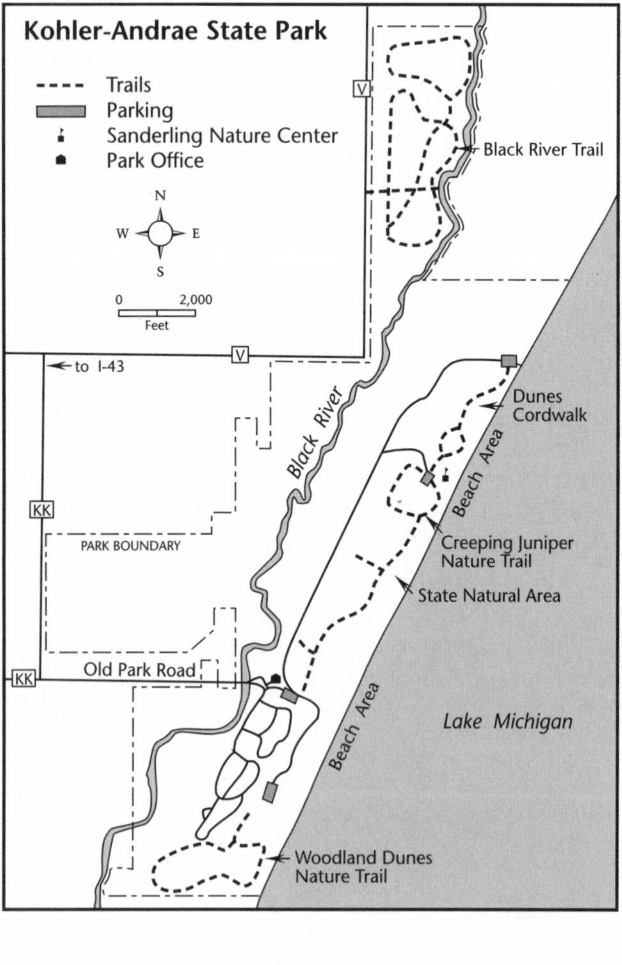

Kohler-Andrae State Park
Trails
Parking
Sanderling Nature Center
Park Office
N
W
E
S
0
2,000
Feet
V
V
to I-43
KK
KK
PARK BOUNDARY
Old Park Road
Black River
Black River Trail
Dunes Cordwalk
Beach Area
Creeping Juniper Nature Trail
State Natural Area
Beach Area
Lake Michigan
Woodland Dunes Nature Trail

2 Cordwalk Trails Go among Protected Sand Dunes

Kohler-Andrae State Park, south of Sheboygan

On the shore of Lake Michigan a state park offers a unique hiking experience among sand dunes in a 135-acre state natural area. Trails atop the undulating surface of stabilized and forming dunes will take you past protected interdunal wetlands, through several small white pine forests, and among "state-threatened" vegetation.

Description and special features. The park contains a trail system within the natural area, a separate nature trail, and a multipurpose trail.

Dunes Cordwalk. A 2.5-mile trail constructed of environmentally friendly cordwalk takes the walker throughout the natural area among the dunes and interdunal wetlands. Builders of the cordwalk string together preservative-treated boards with rope. They then simply lay the cordwalk on the sand. Two scenic overviews with benches provide views of the wetlands and Lake Michigan.

Creeping Juniper Nature Trail. A 0.5 mile of cordwalk loops within the natural area near the Sanderling Nature Center. Information stations on the trail highlight special surface features of the dunes and the rare vegetation that grows on them.

Woodland Dunes Nature Trail. A separate nature trail at the south end of the park goes for 1 mile through a mature forest of pines, maples, birches, basswoods, cottonwoods, oaks, and others. Information stations identify the trees and explain the characteristics of a forest in the "tension zone," which contains trees typical of both northern and southern Wisconsin.

Black River Trail. North of the natural area, a 2.5-mile trail is designed for horseback riding and mountain biking, but may also be used by hikers. It goes through grassland, native wood-lands, and a pine plantation.

Lake Michigan beach area. While not designated as a trail, the 2-mile-long sand beach provides a pleasant lakeside walking experience. You may see a variety of shore birds—including the sanderling, after which the park's nature center is named—that either nest nearby or stop during migrations.

Degree of difficulty. Aside from the mild slopes of dunes, Kohler-Andrae's terrain is mostly flat. The cordwalk in the natural area eases walking in the sand. Other trails have a natural surface.

How to get there. From the intersection of I-43 and County V south of Sheboygan, go east 1 mile on V to County KK, south 1 mile to Old Park Road, then east 0.7 mile to the park entrance. The Black River Trail has a separate entrance. From the intersection of County V and KK, take V east 1 mile, then north 0.7 mile to the trailhead on the right.

Regulations. The park is open to day users from 6:00 A.M. to 11:00 P.M. daily. Walkers must stay on trails in the natural area. Pets must be leashed and are allowed only on the Black River Trail. Trail bikes are also allowed only on the Black River Trail. You will need a state park annual or daily permit for your auto.

Facilities. This full-service park has parking, camping, rest-rooms, playground areas, picnic shelters, and a swimming beach.

Other points of interest in area

The *Sanderling Nature Center* in the park contains murals identifying wildlife and picturing landscapes. A user-operated audio-visual show tells about the evolution of Lake Michigan. Volunteers sell park souvenirs in a small retail shop. Hours are 12:30–4:30 P.M. Wednesday through Sunday, and 1:00–3:00 P.M. Monday and Tuesday, from Memorial Day through Labor Day. In May, September, and October the center is open Saturday and Sunday from 12:30 to 4:30 P.M.

North of the park, at Twelfth and Panther in Sheboygan, *Indian Mound Park* contains two trails. One weaves among 18 effigy and burial mounds. A glassed-in display shows how mound builders buried their dead in a flexed position. A separate nature trail descends into the bottomland adjoining Hartman's Creek. Information stations describe the ecology of the place.

3 Three Northside Parks Offer Walking Variety

Maywood, Evergreen, and Jaycee Parks, Sheboygan

Bordering the banks of the gently flowing Pigeon River, three adjoining parks provide opportunities on 8.6 miles of trails for hikers who like to get vigorous exercise, view wildlife, or just go for an enjoyable walk in the woods.

Description and special features.

Maywood Park. The crown jewel of Sheboygan's park system, the 119-acre Ellwood H. May Environmental Park was willed to the city by its namesake, a local industrialist. You can enjoy four separate hiking experiences on four trails:

Woodland Trail (0.25 mile) goes through a maple forest where sugaring is demonstrated in early spring.

Wetland Trail (0.75 mile) passes ponds and the river. It's a favorite for bird watchers. The wetlands are under development with help from the State Department of Transportation.

Prairie Trail (0.3 mile) goes through 10 acres of developing restored native prairie.

Bluebird Trail (1.75 miles) goes over prairie and past woods. Bluebird boxes along the trail have attracted the eastern bluebird, once plentiful but now scarce in Wisconsin.

Naturalists hold environmental programs in the park and in the Ecology Center for local school children and adults.

Evergreen Park. Tall white pines and other conifers surround the trails in this large recreational park. Upon entering the park from the main entrance on busy, treeless State Highway 42, you're immediately impressed with the transformation of the environment into a forest of towering pines. The park contains picnic shelter houses, baseball diamonds, and a children's playground.

Jaycee Park. A trail goes around an old, water-filled limestone quarry that now has a modern swimming beach including the large "Aqua Avalanche" water slide. The trail begins at the parking lot, goes along the Pigeon River, and loops around the quarry over its bare ledges on the south side. The trail connects to Evergreen and Maywood park trails via a concrete walkway under State Highway 42.

Surfacing varies on these trails. Most have a natural surface. Some have wood chips in moist areas and limestone screenings where there is heavy bike use.

Degree of difficulty. Flat or gently rolling terrain predominates. Because of the development of wetlands, some trails in Maywood are wet or muddy in wet weather. During our spring visit, trail bike ruts were apparent in wet portions of Evergreen.

How to get there. From the intersection of I-43 and State Highway 42 at the northwest corner of Sheboygan, go southeast 0.9 mile on Business 42 to Mueller Road, and west 0.3 mile to Maywood's entrance on the left. Jaycee Park is on the left side of Business 42, 1.4 miles southeast of I-43, and Evergreen Park is on the right side 1.6 miles from the interstate.

Regulations. No pets or collecting are allowed in Maywood. Parks are open 6:00 A.M. to 10:00 P.M. daily. Most trails are open for cross-country skiing.

Facilities. Each park has restrooms and parking. The restrooms in Maywood are in the Ecology Center; in Jaycee Park, in the Quarryview Center. Both Evergreen and Jaycee parks have picnic facilities and playgrounds. Jaycee Park also has a swimming beach.

Other points of interest in area

See pages 127–28 for information about the *Riverfront Boardwalk* and the *Lakefront Multi-purpose Trail*.

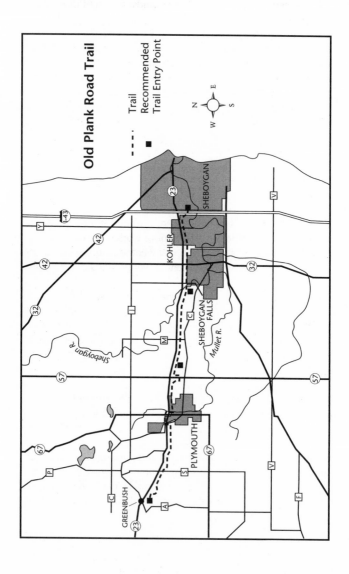

Old Plank Road Trail

- – – – Trail
- ■ Recommended
  Trail Entry Point

4 Seventeen-Mile Asphalt Trail Accommodates Many Users

Old Plank Road Trail, Sheboygan to Greenbush

Native Americans first walked this route on a footpath. Then early white settlers built a plank road for their horses and wagons. Now a 10-foot-wide asphalt trail that parallels State Highway 23 from Sheboygan to Greenbush is multipurpose in every sense of the word. It accommodates walkers, joggers, bicyclists, skaters, and mopeds. Horseback riders use an adjoining mowed strip, and during the winter nordic skiers and snowmobilers are on that strip.

Description and special features. Two inches of asphalt over a 4-inch crushed rock base provide a durable pavement for this 17-mile trail. A lighted tunnel goes under I-43 near the east trailhead, and bridges, one 200 feet long, span two rivers. Started in 1977, the pace of construction quickened in the late 1980s and early 1990s. Total cost, funded by state, county, federal, and private sources, was over $1.2 million.

Degree of difficulty. Rolling terrain makes for only gentle slopes. The trail's 10-foot-wide pavement easily accommodates the variety of users. Several busy road crossings have been regraded to improve traffic safety.

How to get there. The entire trail corridor between the west edge of Sheboygan and Greenbush lies in the state-owned right-of-way of State Highway 23. You may enter the trail anywhere along its length. Park at one of the entry points listed below.

Regulations. Mopeds and snowmobiles are the only motorized vehicles allowed.

Facilities. Entry points with parking and restrooms are located at the west end of Erie Street in Sheboygan, at Meadowlark

Road near Sheboygan Falls, at State Highway 57 near Plymouth, and in Greenbush.

Other points of interest in area

Contact the *Sheboygan County Convention and Visitors Bureau,* 712 River Front Drive, Sheboygan, WI 53081 (phone 800-457-9497), for a brochure describing 30 special attractions in communities along the trail.

For a brochure describing the *Historic Plymouth Walking Tour,* contact the Chamber of Commerce, P.O. Box 584, Plymouth, WI 53073-0584. Phone 414-893-0079.

5 Riverwalk Shows Off Scenic River Rapids

Jaycee Riverwalk, Sheboygan Falls

In the nineteenth century, when Sheboygan Falls was first settled, town pioneers viewed their river from a footpath on the rim of a high bank. Starting in 1992, walkers got a closer look. The local Jaycee chapter raised $20,000 and enlisted the help of the Wisconsin Conservation Corps to build a scenic walkway that cuts into the steep bank. From it you can see the Sheboygan River rapids close up.

Description and special features. Start your walk at the Main Street Bridge near *River Park*. The trail follows a wide bend in the river and ends at the corner of Monroe and Water streets. A spur of wooden stairs climbs the steep bank to provide a second access point farther north on Water Street. The 0.25-mile path has a gravel surface and is shored up on both sides with heavy wooden ties. Wide wooden bridges cross ravines close to the river. Rest on any of several benches at scenic overlooks. Vegetation is mostly young hardwood trees.

Degree of difficulty. Though part of it was cut into a steep bank, the wide trail has only a few steep grades. I advise caution in places where there is a steep drop-off to the side toward the river.

How to get there. From State Highway 23 just west of Kohler, take State Highway 32 south about 2 miles. It becomes Main Street upon entering the city.

Regulations. Pets must be leashed.

Facilities. Just west of the Main Street Bridge is River Park, which has restrooms that are open May 15 through October 15. A footbridge across the river goes to a municipal parking lot next to 375 Buffalo Street. The park, which is open from 6:00

A.M. to 10:00 P.M., also has picnic shelters, tennis courts, and playground equipment.

Other points of interest in area

Settled by German immigrants in the mid-1800s, *Sheboygan Falls* has many restored or preserved buildings and homes in two districts listed in the National Register of Historic Places.

6 Waterfront Revitalization Includes Boardwalk and Trail

Sheboygan Riverfront Boardwalk and Lakefront Multi-Purpose Trail

When you drive through downtown Sheboygan to the waterfront, it's hard to imagine that, just a few years ago, dilapidated houses and abandoned buildings were the norm. Local leaders and citizens have joined hands to transform the river- and lakefronts. They've built an impressive new Harbor Centre Marina and "fishing village" commercial center, attracting new businesses and city dwellers, and revitalizing the entire area. Their plans included the Riverfront Boardwalk for casual strolling and the Lakefront Multi-Purpose Trail for more vigorous walking, jogging, biking, and even in-line skating.

Description and special features.

Riverfront Boardwalk. For about a third of a mile along the bank of the Sheboygan River, the boardwalk reminds the stroller of San Francisco's Fisherman's Wharf because it attracts arts-and-crafts vendors and even fishing charter boats. Restaurants and gift and antique shops replaced riverside shanties. But designers retained the weathered, bare-wood waterfront appearance. Warm weather attracts crowds and increased commercial activity, but on a cool spring or fall walk you can share the quiet with the inevitable sea gulls and terns.

Lakefront Multi-Purpose Trail. Going close to the shore for 1.5 miles from the public launch, through Deland Community Park and past its inviting swimming beach to North Point Park, this wide concrete and asphalt trail provides room for every type of unmotorized locomotion—walking, jogging, biking, skating. You can also enjoy Lake Michigan's seaside atmosphere while walking out on a new connecting breakwater that encloses the 400-boat Harbor Centre Marina.

Degree of difficulty. Easy, level surfaces characterize both the boardwalk and the multipurpose trail.

How to get there. The boardwalk follows the bank of the Sheboygan River between the Eighth Street Bridge and the intersection of Pennsylvania Avenue and North Fifth Street in downtown Sheboygan. The multipurpose trail parallels Broughton Drive from just north of Pennsylvania Avenue to North Point Drive.

Regulations. No pets are allowed on the boardwalk. Bikes must be walked. No motorized vehicles are permitted on either trail.

Facilities. You'll find restrooms in restaurants on the boardwalk, in the Harbor Centre building, and at the beach in Deland Park. You may park in areas between River Front Drive and the boardwalk and at several lots in the Harbor Centre.

Other points of interest in area

In downtown Sheboygan at 608 New York Avenue, the *J. M. Kohler Arts Center* offers visual and performing arts in a restored home and gallery. The center is open daily 10:00 A.M. to 5:00 P.M., and also 7:00 to 9:00 P.M. on Mondays. It's closed holidays.

Milwaukee Area

There is no better way to recapture the spirit of an era than to follow old trails, gathering from the earth itself the feelings and challenges of those who trod them long ago.

Sigurd F. Olson, OPEN HORIZONS

1. Milwaukee County
2. Ozaukee County
3. Washington County
4. Waukesha County
5. Dodge County

Milwaukee County

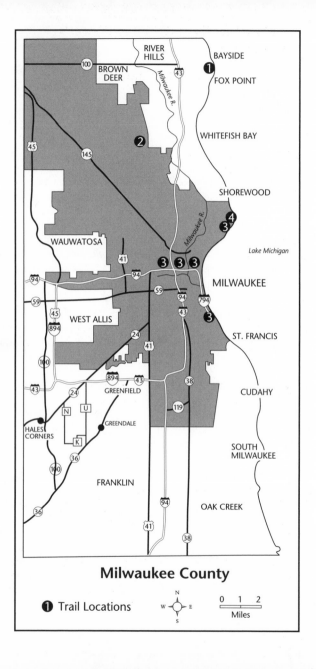

Milwaukee County

1 Trail Locations

1 Nature Sanctuary Occupies Brewer's Former Farm

Schlitz Audubon Center, near Fox Point

Draft horses that hauled wagonloads of Schlitz beer barrels once pastured here. Times and needs changed, and the brewery owners, the Uihlein family, donated the 225-acre farm to the National Audubon Society in 1971. Since then the Schlitz Audubon Center has become a leading source of environmental education in the Milwaukee area. Walk its trails not only for exercise but also to learn about your interdependence with nature.

Description and special features. Five major trails plus a variety of spurs, totaling about 6 miles, reveal the lakeside sanctuary's treasures. Obtain a map and guide at the center's main building.

Green Tree Trail 👟 is a wheelchair-accessible, asphalt-paved double loop. On it, the Tree-Top Classroom, a tall wood tower, provides a sweeping view of the preserve and Lake Michigan.

Beach Loop 👟 👟 follows the Lake Michigan shore on a flat, ancient terrace at the base of the bluff. The cool, windy, lakeside microclimate creates an environment for conifer trees usually found farther north. A wide, asphalt path down the bluff provides easy access to the lake and trail.

Ravine Loops 👟 👟 follow a twisting route for about 0.8 mile through woods of birch and other trees along the rims of deep ravines formed by rainwater run-off toward the lake. In the ravines, notice concrete dams built years ago to retard erosion.

Grassland Loops 👟 👟 meander through a meadow. Just to the left of the trailhead, a spur goes to a boardwalk that crosses a small pond, where you may see painted turtles sunning themselves on logs. The trail also takes you to several ponds and a bird blind to observe waterfowl from concealment.

Woodland Loop can be reached by means of stairs and a bridge across a deep ravine. The 0.9-mile trail follows the rim of the ravine through birch woods, and then loops away from the ravine through pine and mixed hardwoods, returning to the stairs. From this loop, a trail back to the center building takes you near the Mystery Pond. You can rest and observe wildlife from a bench atop a pond-side mound.

Degree of difficulty. The gently undulating terrain of the center provides for trails with few slopes. Except for the asphalt Green Tree Trail, trails are natural, usually grassy surface or covered with wood chips. Maintenance is good, though we encountered a few muddy spots during our spring walk. The current condition of the trails is posted on a board in the center building.

How to get there. From I-43 north of Milwaukee, take Brown Deer Road east 1.4 miles to the entrance on the right.

Regulations. Members of Friends of Schlitz Audubon Center are admitted free. Annual membership is a minimum of $25 per individual or $35 per family. The daily entrance fee is $2 per person for nonmembers. No collecting, pets, smoking, swimming, or picnicking is allowed in the center. Biking is permitted only on the main road to the parking lot. You may cross-country ski on some trails, though they are not groomed. The sanctuary is open from 9:00 A.M. to 5:00 P.M. Tuesday through Sunday and is closed Monday.

Facilities. The center's main building has restrooms and a drinking fountain, as well as environmental exhibits, a book store, and an information counter. It also houses classrooms and administrative offices.

Other points of interest in area

For those who wish to visit Schlitz Audubon Center but also would like to picnic, swim, or take the children to a playground, *Doctor's Park* offers these opportunities. It is located on Lake Michigan just south of the center. From Brown Deer Road just west of the center, go south on Lake Drive and east on Dean Road to the park's entrance.

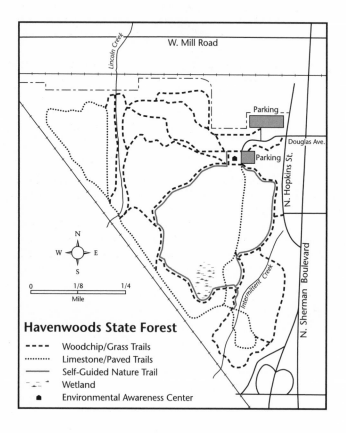

Havenwoods State Forest

- - - - Woodchip/Grass Trails
.... Limestone/Paved Trails
———— Self-Guided Nature Trail
- ˙- ‾ Wetland
● Environmental Awareness Center

2 Self-Guiding Nature Trail Reveals Restored Green Space

Havenwoods State Forest, Milwaukee

Urban development gobbles up land. But in a few places people are reclaiming abused land and restoring it to the natural community. Havenwoods, a 237-acre green oasis in the midst of the city, is such a place. Its checkered past includes uses as a farm, a prison, a landfill, and a guided-missile site. Since acquiring Havenwoods, the state Department of Natural Resources' program of healing has included the planting of some 40,000 trees and many wildflowers, restoring prairie, digging a pond for wildlife, and building some 7 miles of walking trails.

Description and special features. While a variety of trails wander through the property, the 1.4-mile Self-Guiding Nature Trail provides the best walking experience. It takes the walker to the main features of the property, including the Wild Goose Pond, the sites of the old prison and farm, and the restored prairie. A printed guide, keyed to numbered stakes on the trail, tells about the history of the place and points out how the restored land has attracted wildlife.

Degree of difficulty. The Self-Guiding Nature Trail loops over mostly level terrain through large clearings and some woodland. It has a natural, mowed surface.

How to get there. At 6141 North Hopkins Street, Havenwoods is on the city's north side just south of Mill Road and west of Sherman Boulevard.

Regulations. Trails are open from 6:00 A.M. to 8:00 P.M. daily. The main building, the Environmental Awareness Center, is open Monday through Friday, 7:45 A.M. to 4:30 P.M., and on weekends when special programs are held. Pets must be leashed. Bicycles are allowed only on limestone-paved paths.

137

No motorized vehicles, fires, firearms, or alcoholic beverages are allowed. The state forest maintains 2.5 miles of cross-country ski trails in winter. A state park permit is not required.

Facilities. The Environmental Awareness Center contains restrooms, a lending library for teachers and the public, an auditorium and classroom, an exhibit area, and administrative offices. While Havenwoods is not a desirable picnicking destination, a few picnic tables are provided near the parking lots.

Other points of interest in area

Milwaukee County's *Brown Deer Park* nearby offers additional hiking trails, picnic shelters, other recreational facilities, and restrooms. This large park has entrances on Green Bay Avenue, North Range Line Road, Calumet Road, and West Bradley Road.

3 Visit the Past while Walking in the Present

Historical Building Tours, Milwaukee

In the nineteenth century, when Germans, Poles, Irish, Italians, and others immigrated to Milwaukee, they brought their cultures with them, making the city rich in ethnic diversity. The homes, churches, and commercial buildings they built replicate the styles of their European homelands. Settlers from Germany, in particular, left their mark on city architecture. Many of these structures have been preserved, and the designs of newer buildings among them often reflect the older styles.

Self-guiding walking and driving tours, described in brochures available through the Department of City Development, highlight the unique and best-preserved homes and buildings. Each of 10 brochures (with more to come) provides a neighborhood map showing the itinerary and a key to brief histories of featured structures.

Obtain a free set at the City Hall from the Historical Preservation Commission, Department of City Development, 809 North Broadway, Milwaukee, WI 53201-0324. Phone 414-286-5705.

Description and special features.

Following are several of the tours described in the brochures:

Avenues West (40 blocks) covers a rectangle bordered by North Eleventh Street, West Wisconsin Avenue, North Twenty-fifth Street, and West Highland Avenue, and includes a major portion of the Marquette University campus. Among buildings on the tour are Captain Frederick Pabst's mansion, a prime example of German-inspired architecture and now a museum; the Eagle's Club, once an important social center; and Marquette University's St. Joan of Arc Chapel, a fifteenth-century church moved block-by-block from France and reconstructed.

Bay View (82 blocks). Once an incorporated village centered on an iron mill south of the Kinnickinnic River, this lakeside community was annexed by Milwaukee in 1887. The ironworks are gone, but Bay View retains its independent character, which the tour highlights. Because of this tour's length, you may want to walk portions where important sites are clustered, and drive elsewhere. You'll see the Rolling Mill Historical Marker, homes of former mill workers and village merchants, and the former artesian Pryor Avenue Well, now mechanically pumped, where residents still fill their jugs with fresh spring water.

Juneautown (two tours comprising 30 blocks). Milwaukee originated at this east-side downtown location, named after the first Caucasian settler, Solomon Juneau. Walking tours take you past a mix of elegantly restored historical buildings and prestigious modern addresses. You'll view St. Mary's Church, which is the city's oldest building, the Pabst Theater, a restored brewery, and commercial buildings. Be sure to go inside the City Hall, completed in 1895, and see its unique skylit atrium. The tours include the Milwaukee County War Memorial and Art Museum, a lakeside building of catilevered concrete and glass.

North Point (24 blocks). If you like to stroll quiet, tree-lined sidewalks and view beautiful old houses, this tour will delight you. Centered on a Gothic water tower built in 1873 on the city's near northeast side, the North Point neighborhood attracted wealthy local industrialists and merchants in the late nineteenth and early twentieth centuries. They retained some of the nation's leading architects for their homes near the newly established Lake Park (see pp. 142–43). Highlights include the Gustave and Hilda Pabst House, an imposing Classical Revival mansion, and the Frederick C. Bogk House, designed by Frank Lloyd Wright. North Point is a local historic district, and a portion is listed in the National Register of Historic Places.

Kilbourntown (21 blocks). Byron Kilbourn established this community in the 1830s just west of the Milwaukee River opposite Juneautown as the latter's rival. While many original buildings have given way to freeways and construction of the Civic Center and County Court House, some older structures remain. The area is a center of retailing, convention, and sports activities. Along the way, you will view Old World Third Street, an area of restored commercial buildings now housing shops and restaurants. The indoor Grand Avenue Mall links six historical buildings and is a center of downtown shopping. Donated by the Petit family and built in 1986–88, the Bradley Center is home to the Milwaukee Bucks and Marquette University basketball teams.

Yankee Hill (20 blocks). One of Milwaukee's earliest residential neighborhoods, Yankee Hill was originally much larger than it is today. Freeway construction and urban renewal reduced its size, and pressure for higher-density land use changed its character from single-family homes to a mix of apartments and commercial buildings. But many buildings from the late 1800s remain. The tour includes several cathedrals and other churches, nineteenth-century row houses, and a variety of elegant old homes.

Degree of difficulty. Tours are easy to walk along city streets. Some Milwaukee neighborhoods are in a state of social and economic transition. When walking in these areas, you are advised to exercise the same caution regarding personal safety that you would observe in any unfamiliar surroundings.

How to get there. In southeastern Wisconsin, Milwaukee can be reached via Interstate Highways 94 and 43.

Regulations. Walkers are cautioned to observe crosswalk signs and lights. Traffic is heavy, particularly in downtown Milwaukee.

Facilities. You can park on streets in designated areas in all neighborhoods and in parking ramps downtown.

4 Bluff-top Path Provides Sweeping Lake Views

Lake Park, northeast Milwaukee

Bluff top

Ravines

In 1890–92, the city's newly created Park Commission acquired parcels of land on a bluff overlooking Lake Michigan. This assured lake access in the future for the prestigious North Point neighborhood. To lay out the grounds, the commission hired Frederick Law Olmsted, who had been codesigner of New York City's Central Park.

Ravines running toward the lake slice through the bluff-top park, making for a variety of terrain. Tall trees and level grassy areas form a traditional parklike atmosphere on top of the bluff. Ravines are wooded and narrow with steep walls and small creeks that run occasionally, especially in spring.

Description and special features. Wide asphalt walks lace the upper park. One that runs along the brow of the bluff affords sweeping views of the lake. Concrete bridges, some guarded by sandstone lions, span the ravines. Along the path you'll see an impressive statue of Brigadier General Erastus B. Wolcott, Wisconsin's surgeon general during the Civil War, on his mount. The park's pavilion, built in 1902, now houses a restaurant. Also on this path is an iron lighthouse that was moved to this location in 1879.

A second asphalt path runs along North Wahl Avenue and North Lake Street across the street from a number of architecturally unique homes, many nearly a century old, built by early Milwaukee industrialists and merchants.

A path runs along the bottom of each ravine, with wooden bridges crossing the creek beds. Steep steps made of inlaid wooden ties descend into some of the ravines.

An asphalt path follows a portion of the bottom of the bluff and is often preferred by walkers to the lakeside path on the east side of Lincoln Memorial Drive. The latter has much busier bicycle and in-line skater traffic.

Degree of difficulty. Bluff-top asphalt paths are generally wide and level, literally "a walk in the park." During my early spring walk I found the ravine trails to be muddy and trash-strewn, with some bridges in poor repair. (No doubt the county's maintenance crew hadn't had a chance yet to perform spring clean-up and repair.)

How to get there. Lake Park, on the city's near northeast side, is east of Lake Drive and Wahl Avenue between East North Avenue and East Kenwood Boulevard.

Regulations. The park is open from sunrise until 10:00 P.M. No dogs are permitted. Alcohol may not be brought into the park except with an alcohol permit during special events.

Facilities. Recreational facilities include a pitch-and-putt golf course, a Vita exercise course, playground equipment, picnic areas, lawn bowling, shuffleboard, a softball diamond, and lighted tennis courts. The park also has restrooms and parking.

Other points of interest in area

Bradford Beach, a popular Lake Michigan swimming beach, is across Lincoln Memorial Drive from Lake Park. The publicly owned lakeshore stretches about 3 miles from Juneau Park in downtown Milwaukee, northeast to the water purification plant. It affords opportunities for boating, fishing, jogging, biking, and skating, as well as swimming and walking.

Ozaukee County

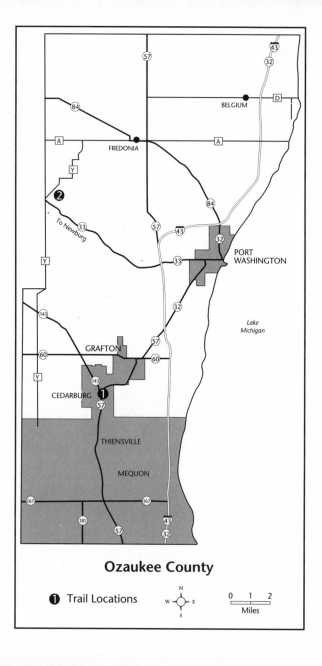

Ozaukee County

1 Trail Locations

0 1 2
Miles

N
W E
S

1 Walk through Yesterday in Downtown Cedarburg

Washington Avenue Historic District, Cedarburg

German and Irish pioneers who settled near Cedar Creek in the 1840s built log cabins along Washington Avenue. But when the railroad came in 1870, it brought many visitors and salesmen and booming commercial activity. Two local quarries provided the Niagara limestone for many of the more durable homes, hotels, and shops.

Most of these buildings are still standing. They make up the Washington Avenue Historic District, which is listed on the National Register of Historic Places.

The local Landmarks Commission designed a walking tour through the district, and with the Chamber of Commerce published a booklet in which the old buildings are featured.

Description and special features. Most of the 59 preserved structures line Washington Avenue in the heart of the downtown. Following are some of the highlights:

Woolen mill buildings on the north end of downtown composed an entire industry, powered by a dam on Cedar Creek. Restoration began in 1972, and now the buildings form a complex called Cedar Creek Settlement. They house a variety of shops.

The Charles Gottlieb Friederich Cobbler Shop and residence, W63 N670-2 Washington Avenue, is a 2½-story building constructed of cream city brick. Elliptical brick arches over windows and doors add distinction.

The Milwaukee Northern Bridge, south of Advent Lutheran Church, carried the interurban, rapid-transit trains across Cedar Creek. Now it's a footbridge.

Cedarburg Mill, N58 W6181 Columbia Road, a five-story stone grist mill, dominated the area. The lower walls of this limestone building are 32 inches thick. Residents sought safety here in 1862 during an "Indian scare."

Wadham's Pagoda Filling Station, next to the mill, is a prime example of a contrasting style. Wadham's Oil and Grease Company of Milwaukee built more than 100 of these oriental-style filling stations.

Leopold Jochem residence, W63 N675 Washington Avenue, is the largest late-Victorian mansion in Cedarburg. Jochem mixed the Queen Anne and Classical Revival styles and built with pressed brick.

Degree of difficulty. You'll follow the tour on city sidewalks. The only hazard to walkers is the traffic at crossings.

How to get there. Cedarburg is at the junction of State Highways 57 and 143 in Ozaukee County.

Regulations. None. Obviously, you'll get the most enjoyment from this tour during daylight hours. You can buy the brochure describing the tour for a small fee at the Chamber of Commerce office in the City Hall, W63 N645 Washington Avenue. It's open Monday through Friday 8:30–11:00 A.M. and 12:30–4:30 P.M.

Facilities. You may park along Washington Avenue. Restrooms are available in the City Hall, mentioned above.

Other points of interest in area

Walk across the last original covered bridge in Wisconsin, located in *Covered Bridge Park,* 3 miles north of Cedarburg. The park also offers picnic tables, grills, restrooms, and drinking water. Take State Highway 143 north to its junction with State Highway 60 and Covered Bridge Road. Go north on Covered Bridge Road to the park.

2 Fifteen Trails Lace Environmental Learning Place

Riveredge Nature Center, Newburg

This nature sanctuary can perhaps best be described as a University of the Environment. A full-time staff and platoons of volunteers offer courses, workshops, field trips, and so on, of every conceivable type related to the interdependence of humankind and the natural world. It has become a major educational resource for Milwaukee-area schools and adult groups. A variety of trails shows off the diversity of wild things in its 350 acres.

Description and special features. I was able to walk only a sampling of Riveredge's 15 trails during my June visit. I gleaned the following descriptions from the center's literature. Since most trails are short and interconnected, you can walk several in a couple hours while looping back to your starting point. Teacher-naturalist Mary Holleback provided difficulty ratings.

Trail numbers below are keyed to the map shown here, which is based on the map available at the center's main building.

1. Prairie Trail 👟 👟 (0.24 mile). See prairie grasses and wildflowers, as well as a "succession" demonstration.

2. Trillium Trail 👟 👟 👟 👟 (0.19 mile). Many trilliums along this forested path in spring and migrating birds both spring and fall make this trail a naturalist's favorite.

3. River Trail 👟 👟 👟 (0.5 mile). This scenic riverside trail passes over a glacial kame and through white cedar and birch woods.

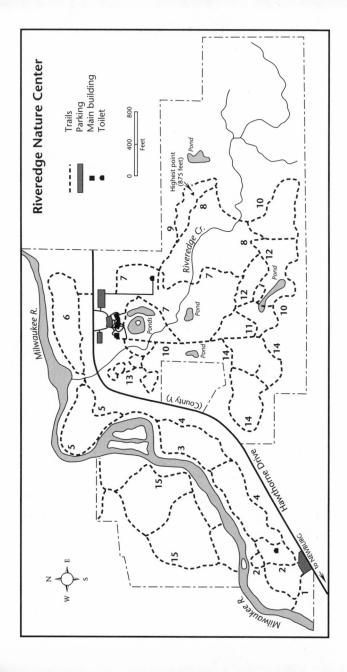

Riveredge Nature Center

Trails
Parking
Main building
Toilet

Feet
0 400 800

Milwaukee R.

Riveredge Cr.

Highest point
(875 feet)

Pond

Pond

Pond

Ponds

Pond

Pond

(County Y)

Hawthorne Drive

to NEWBURG

Milwaukee R.

N
W E
S

6
7
7
7
9
8
8
10
12
7
12
10
11
14
14
13
10
5
5
4
3
15
15
4
14
2
1

4. Forest Trail 👟 👟 👟 👟 (0.59 mile). The trail goes through a climax forest of maple, beech, elm, and basswood.

5. Marsh Trail 👟 👟 👟 (0.67 mile). View many native birds on the path and a boardwalk through a river floodplain and marsh.

6. Oak Trail 👟 👟 👟 (0.65 mile). See many wildflowers and the ostrich fern along this wooded walk.

7. Ecology Trail 👟 👟 👟 (0.9 mile). This trail is a naturalist's dream because of the variety of plant communities along the path and boardwalk.

8. Grasshopper Trail 👟 👟 👟 (0.55 mile). View old field succession on this path through extensive grasslands.

9. Outlook Trail 👟 👟 👟 👟 (0.27 mile). Climb a glacial moraine to the center's highest point (875 feet above sea level).

10. Bluebird Trail 👟 👟 (1.02 miles). You may see bluebirds nesting in boxes in meadows on this trail.

11. Rabbit Run 👟 👟 👟 (0.23 mile). Compare different kinds of grass in prairie grass seed production strips planted here.

12. Swamp Walk 👟 👟 👟 (0.3 mile). View aquatic animals from a floating boardwalk that crosses a vernal pond.

13. Maple Trail 👟 👟 👟 (0.47 mile). Maples on this trail provide sap for syrup in early spring.

14. Raptor Run 👟 👟 👟 (0.59 mile). The red-shouldered hawk and Cooper's hawk live in the hardwood forest this path goes through.

15. Big Oak Trail 👟 👟 👟 👟 (1.4 miles). The center plans to build a bridge to this trail that meanders through a forest on the northwest side of the Milwaukee River. Until then, ask a staff member how to reach it.

Degree of difficulty. Paths are well maintained with either a natural or wood chip surface. Portions may be muddy in wet weather, especially near the river. The undulating terrain has many gentle slopes and a few steep ones. While many trails are not marked, there are a few maps posted at strategic intersections.

How to get there. From State Highway 33 in Newburg, take County Y (Hawthorne Drive) 1.2 miles northeast to the entrance on the right.

Regulations. Trails are open throughout the year from dawn to dusk. Hours for the main building are 8:00 A.M. to 5:00 P.M. Monday through Friday, and noon to 4:00 P.M. Saturday during the school year (closed then in summer) and Sunday all year. Fees for nonmembers are $1.50 for adults and $1 for children ages 3–18. Younger children are admitted free. Annual memberships are available.

Riveredge prohibits biking, smoking, pets, picnics, and collecting.

Facilities. In the main building you'll find restrooms, a water fountain, a book store, classrooms, and nature displays. You'll also find a drinking fountain outside the main building and several pit toilets on trails.

Other points of interest in area.

On Highway 33, 2.5 miles southeast of Newburg, a trail goes into the *Cedarburg Bog State Natural Area.* The limestone-covered path goes about a third of a mile to a small lake. Along the trail you may see protected, rare wetland plant species. Park in a small lot at the trailhead on the south side of the road.

Washington County

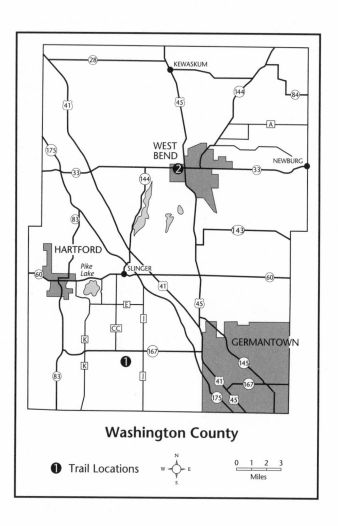

Washington County

1 Trail Locations

N
W ⊕ E
S

0 1 2 3
Miles

1 You Could Hike the Kettle Moraine at Your Wedding

Glacier Hills County Park, southeast of Hartford

A 140-acre park in the kettle moraine region of southern Washington County offers hiking opportunities on four trails. You can also play volleyball and basketball, picnic, go swimming, or even get married in a rustic chapel in this park.

Description and special features. Hike through thick forests, over meadows, or into a dense pine plantation on these trails.

Black Trail 👟 👟 👟 👟 (1.1 miles) follows high ridges through a mostly deciduous forest to a pond, and then to Friess Lake. Indigo buntings and scarlet tanagers have been spotted along this trail and the Red Trail.

Red Trail 👟 👟 👟 👟 (0.9 mile) is conterminous with the Black Trail until it branches off and climbs a kame. It also passes a deep marsh kettle known as St. Aemelian's Bog, where the pitcher plant and other rare bog species are known to grow.

Green Trail 👟 👟 👟 (1 mile) goes through a small valley with a plantation of Norway spruce so dense it blocks the sun and cools the air perceptibly.

Blue Trail 👟 👟 👟 (0.7 mile) meanders over a grassy clearing and through newly established woodland.

Degree of difficulty. The Black and Red trails course up and down steep inclines on top of the kettle moraine. They have a crushed rock or natural surface. The Green and Blue trails start on a hill and descend into a valley on a mowed grass surface. The spruce plantation grows on mostly level land, and here the trail surface is bare.

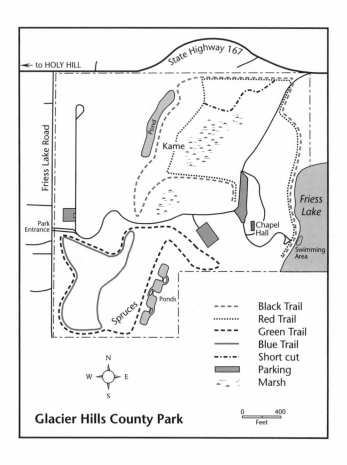

Glacier Hills County Park

Legend:
- – – – Black Trail
- ········ Red Trail
- – – – Green Trail
- ——— Blue Trail
- –·–·– Short cut
- ▓ Parking
- Marsh

0 — 400 Feet

N W E S

How to get there. Glacier Hills County Park is on the east side of Friess Lake Road 0.3 mile south of State Highway 167. The Red and Black trails start from the main parking lot. The Green and Blue coterminous trailhead is near the park's entrance.

Regulations. Park hours are 7:00 A.M. to 9:00 P.M. daily. No bikes or horses are allowed on the trails. You may cross-country ski, but trails are not groomed. Snowmobiles may use separate trails where signs indicate.

Facilities. This well-equipped park has picnic shelters, including a large hall which may be rented. There are basketball and volleyball courts and a small swimming area, but no sand beach. Restrooms and drinking fountains are in the main building, and a pit toilet is located near the lake. A chapel on the grounds may be rented for weddings.

Other points of interest in area

About 2 miles east of the park just south of State Highway 167 on Carmel Road, *Holy Hill* is a Catholic shrine and popular tourist stop. Atop a high moulin kame, the twin spires of the National Shrine of St. Mary can be seen for miles. There is also a gift shop and restaurant on site, and a segment of the Ice Age National Scenic Trail crosses the hill.

2 Trail Follows High Moraines and Eskers

West Bend segment, Ice Age National Scenic Trail

Trails over moraines, kames, and eskers provide some of the best hiking in eastern Wisconsin. A segment of the Ice Age National Scenic Trail along the western edge of West Bend follows a line of ridges and hills deposited by the Laurentide Ice Sheet when it melted.

Description and special features. From its southern trailhead at Paradise Drive, just southwest of the city, the trail crosses grassy private land and enters the Girl Scouts' Camp Silverbrook at its southwest corner. Hikers follow the southern border of the camp and pass to the south of a moderately high kame. Heading northwest, hikers must ford Silver Creek, which, with the bordering marsh, can be as wide as 30 feet in the spring. The trail continues northeast and then turns north along the western edge of the camp and onto a moraine.

Just north of Camp Silverbrook, the trail enters Ridge Run County Park and crosses a kettle by way of a boardwalk. It then goes north along the edge of a glacial ridge and bends around the north end of the ridge, exiting onto University Drive at its intersection with Chestnut Street.

Go north on University Drive, across Washington Avenue, then west about half a block to Wendy's and Culver's Custard restaurants. The off-road trail resumes, climbing the steep southern end of an esker behind Culver's. Watch for a trailhead sign on top of the hill. Going north along the esker, the trail crosses Park Avenue and descends into a valley between ridges just south of Beaver Dam Road.

North of this road, hikers enter Glacial Blue Ridge Recreation Area, an undeveloped West Bend park. The trail continues north along the moraine and ends at County D, the north trailhead.

Degree of difficulty. Though the trail is within or near the city, portions of it are as strenuous as nearly any back-country trail described in this book. The moraines and eskers it follows involve steep slopes and, often, a rocky path. The unimproved stream crossing in Camp Silverbrook offers a special challenge, especially during wet weather.

On the plus side, this Ice Age Trail segment provides great exercise and beautiful glacially formed surroundings, much of which are forested.

How to get there. The following locations provide trail entry with parking nearby: Ridge Run County Park, University Drive across from Chestnut Street (to the west at the end of a short gravel driveway), behind Culver's Custard off Washington Avenue, at Park Avenue, at Beaver Dam Road where the trail enters Glacial Blue Ridge Recreation Area from the south, and at County D. There is no parking at the Paradise Drive trailhead.

Regulations. Horses are prohibited on the entire trail. Ridge Run County Park is open daily from 7:00 A.M. to 9:00 P.M. Dogs must be leashed in the Girl Scout camp and in the park.

Facilities. Ridge Run County Park has restrooms, drinking water (at the north parking lot), picnic areas, and playgrounds. There is a portable toilet next to the parking lot in Glacial Blue Ridge Recreation Area near where the trail enters from the south.

Other points of interest in area

You can learn to hike on a trail or cross country without getting lost by practicing on an orienteering course at *Glacial Blue Ridge Recreation Area*. Start from the parking lot off Beaver Dam Road. Obtain a compass and map at the park system office, 1115 South Main Street. Phone 414-335-5080.

Waukesha County

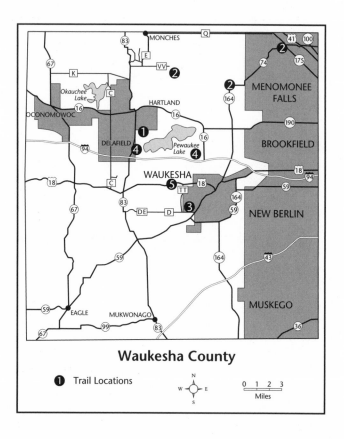

Waukesha County

1 Trail Locations

N
W — E
S

0 1 2 3
Miles

1 Walk a Loop through a Glacial Spillway

Bark River Ice Age Trail, Hartland

When the Laurentide Ice Sheet melted some 12,000 years ago, its meltwater gouged out giant spillways. Now often a river, a remnant of its Ice Age ancestor, meanders between the spillway's wide, steep banks. The Bark River is such a remnant. Its adjoining bottomland is filled with till, boulders, and perhaps even buried kames the glacier left behind.

Description and special features. A segment of the Ice Age National Scenic Trail loops through some 90 acres donated by developers of the Bark River Commerce Center. The trail goes through swampland, over an "island" that may be a buried kame, and along the base of the southern bank of the spillway. A portion crosses an oak savanna of majestic white and burr oaks, some perhaps 200 years old. Information posts identify trees and other biological features.

Degree of difficulty. Terrain is mostly flat or very mildly sloping. About 1,500 feet of boardwalk cross wetlands and small streams. The remainder of the trail has natural surface, some of which may be muddy in wet weather.

How to get there. From I-94 in Waukesha County go north on State Highway 83 for 2.4 miles, then east on Walnut Ridge Drive. There are trail entry points behind each of the three office buildings on the north side of the street. You may park in the back parking lot of the Fotodyne Building along the row of spaces on the east edge of the lot, or park along the street and walk to the back of the property.

Regulations. No bicycles are allowed. Owners of the private property that borders the trail wish to discourage skateboarding, in-line skating, using private dumpsters, picnicking, and dogs. The trail will be accessible as long as users respect those wishes.

Facilities. There are no public facilities.

Other points of interest in area

There are additional hiking trails, through kettle moraine terrain, in the *Penbrook Park Conservancy Area* in Hartland. On Highway 83 go an additional 0.7 mile north from Walnut Ridge Drive to Cardinal Lane, then east to a T-intersection at Maple Avenue, then south 0.1 mile to a trailhead on the left.

2 Trail Follows Abandoned Railroad between Quarries

Bugline Recreation Trail, Menomonee Falls–Merton

In the late 1800s Joseph Hadfield built a railroad in northern Waukesha County to haul stone from the area's quarries. The county acquired most of the right-of-way in 1978 and started work on a trail for bicycle riders and hikers. The resulting 12.2-mile multipurpose trail runs from Menomonee Falls to Merton. Users view urban and rural landscape, including many farms, five quarries, wetlands, a nature preserve, and several parks.

Description and special features. Starting at State Highway 175 in Menomonee Falls, the trail goes south and then east through Lannon. Notice the many homes in Lannon constructed of the distinctive "Lannon stone," quarried nearby. The trail then proceeds to Sussex. En route it passes five major stone quarries and goes along the border of Menomonee Park. Just north of Sussex it passes Coolings Meadows, a nature preserve.

A short break at the Cannery in Sussex takes users along local streets. Traveling toward Merton, take Waukesha Avenue to Silver Spring Drive, then west to Main Street. If you're going toward Menomonee Falls, go east on Main Street to Waukesha Avenue, and then north. Follow directional signs.

Near the west limits of Sussex the trail passes Sussex Village Park, and then the Town of Lisbon Park 1 mile east of Merton. It then skirts the Mill Pond, a flowage of the Bark River. The trailhead in Merton is at County VV.

Degree of difficulty. With a crushed limestone surface, the trail is level, well marked, and easy to walk or bicycle.

How to get there. You can enter the trail at either trailhead, any crossroad, or from any of the parks it passes. Because of

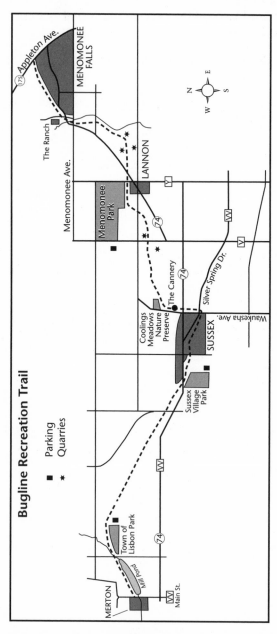

Bugline Recreation Trail

Parking ■
Quarries *

MENOMONEE FALLS

Appleton Ave.

(175)

The Ranch

Menomonee Ave.

LANNON

Menomonee Park

(74)

Coolings Meadows Nature Preserve

The Cannery

Silver Spring Dr.

Waukesha Ave.

SUSSEX

Sussex Village Park

(74)

Town of Lisbon Park

(74)

Mill Pond

MERTON

Main St.

168

its many facilities, Menomonee Park just north of Lannon is a favorite entry point.

Regulations. The trail is open to bicycles, walkers, joggers, and cross-country skiers, though it is not groomed. Horses are allowed on an adjacent bridle trail between the Ranch in Menomonee Falls and Lannon. Snowmobilers may use the trail between Menomonee Avenue near the Ranch and Waukesha Avenue in Sussex. No other motor vehicles are allowed. Dogs must be leashed. You may park on the street where signs permit at trailheads or crossroads, or in parking lots in parks near the trail.

Facilities. In parks as follows:

Menomonee Park: parking, restrooms, picnicking, swimming, hiking, and fishing. *Sussex Village Park:* parking, picnic tables, and shelter buildings. *Town of Lisbon Park:* parking, toilets, picnic tables.

Other points of interest in area

For a back-country hiking experience through a glacially formed river valley, the *Monches segment of the Ice Age National Scenic Trail* follows the Oconomowoc River northeast of Merton. The main trailhead is in Monches near the north Waukesha County line.

3 Boardwalk Penetrates Marsh Teeming with Wildlife

Fox River Sanctuary Trail, Waukesha

As development has encroached on open spaces in Waukesha, city leaders and the state have taken steps to restore and preserve some irreplaceable natural areas. The Fox River Sanctuary is one of these. A wheelchair-accessible boardwalk takes school children and the public into the heart of a wetland that's alive with birds and other wildlife.

Description and special features. Starting from a small parking lot off Sunset Drive on the city's southwest side, the 5-foot-wide boardwalk goes through a cattail marsh and passes several ponds that have been created to attract waterfowl. The 0.25-mile walk then connects to a network of paths that borders the river or goes through wooded bottomland. During my walk in May, I spotted more than a dozen different species of waterfowl and other birds. An elevated platform overlooks the marsh for better viewing of wildlife.

Degree of difficulty. The boardwalk is wide and level, with railings and bumpers on both sides to guide wheelchairs. The connecting paths along the river, which have a grassy surface, slope very little. Portions may be muddy, or even submerged, during wet springtime weather.

How to get there. From its intersection with St. Paul Avenue (County X) in southwest Waukesha, take Sunset Drive (County D) east across the Fox River Bridge. The trailhead parking lot is on the left near the bridge.

Regulations. Dogs must be leashed in the sanctuary.

Facilities. Parking.

Other points of interest in area

The *Glacial Drumlin Trail,* a 46-mile biking and hiking trail, begins in Waukesha at MacArthur Road about a quarter mile west of St. Paul Avenue. The trail follows a former railroad right-of-way through southern Wisconsin to Cottage Grove. On it you'll travel past many drumlins, which are elongated hills left by the Laurentide Ice Sheet.

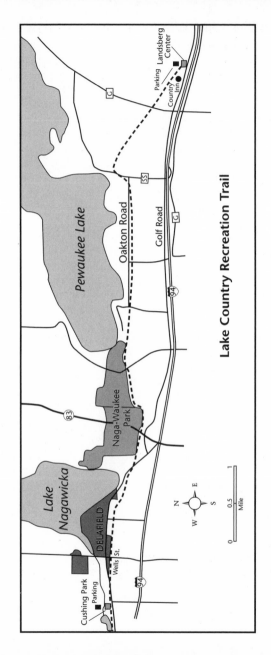

Lake Country Recreation Trail

172

4 Biking and Hiking Trail Connects Lakes and Golf Courses

Lake Country Recreation Trail, Delafield

Business and government worked together to build a bicycling and hiking trail that skirts lakes and golf courses. Businessmen donated the uniquely designed Landsberg barbecue stand for a trailhead center, and it was placed on land donated by a nearby hotel. The electric utility provided right-of-way along an abandoned interurban trolley line. The state and local communities provided funds for trail construction.

Description and special features. The 8-mile trail runs from the Landsberg Center near the Country Inn to just west of Cushing Park in Delafield. It skirts Pewaukee Lake and Lake Nagawicka, as well as three golf courses and a county park. In two places, in the area of County SS and on Wells Street in Delafield, the trail shares the road with motor vehicles.

Degree of difficulty. The trail surface is mostly crushed limestone, with some asphalt, wide and mostly level or gently inclined. Be alert for traffic at crossroads and where the trail shares the road.

How to get there. The Landsberg Center trailhead is on the north frontage road, Golf Road, just east of the County G–I-94 interchange. In Delafield, pick up the trail where it shares Wells Street. A favorite entry point is from Naga-Waukee Park, where camping is allowed. Enter the park from State Highway 83 about 0.5 mile north of I-94.

Regulations. No motor vehicles or horses are allowed on the trail.

Facilities. There are restrooms, parking, and picnic tables at Landsberg Center and at Cushing and Naga-Waukee parks.

Naga-Waukee also has camping, swimming, playground areas, and picnic shelters, as well as a golf course.

Other points of interest in area

Another bicycling and hiking trail, the *New Berlin Recreation Trail*, runs from Greenfield Park in Milwaukee to Springdale Road in Waukesha. This 6-mile trail is also located on right-of-way owned by the Wisconsin Electric Power Company.

5 Leopold's Land Ethic Guides Nature Center

Retzer Nature Center, Waukesha

Aldo Leopold said of his exhausted sand-county farm, ". . . we try to rebuild, with shovel and axe, what we are losing elsewhere." This could be said of Retzer Nature Center. A preserved wilderness it is not. It is, rather, several parcels of land, once in various stages of degradation, that human hands are working to restore. And it has become a place where visitors can learn the ingredients of a natural biotic community and how to restore and respect their own land.

The trails at Retzer show nature in great variety and provide lessons in Leopold's land ethic.

Description and special features. Many of the seven hiking trails have information stations keyed to descriptive literature available at a trailhead dispenser. Center supervisor Larry Kascht helped me with trail descriptions and difficulty ratings.

The Adventure Trail (0.2 mile—orange markers) is a showplace of accessibility. An asphalt, 8.5-foot-wide path has a handrail for support and metal curb to guide those in wheelchairs. Thirty information stations in both raised print and braille describe existing natural features and plans for the trail. Obtain a trail guide, available as a booklet or an audio cassette, at the nature center.

The Self-Guiding Nature Trail (0.45 mile—red markers) goes over old farm fields, through second-growth forest and tree plantations, and near a small pond and marsh. Information stations identify both natural and exotic plants.

The Prairie Vista Trail (0.3 mile—yellow markers) loops over old farm fields now restored to prairie. The prairie units, some of which are 20 years old, demonstrate how various kinds of management affect restoration. The trail begins atop a drumlin with a wide view of the countryside.

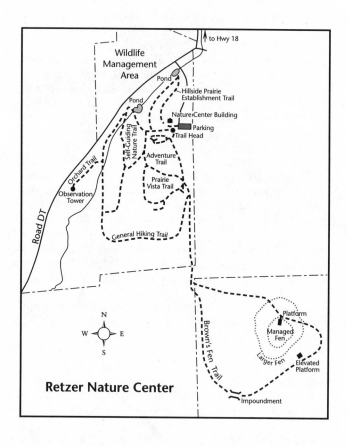

to Hwy 18

Wildlife
Management
Area

Pond

Hillside Prairie
Establishment Trail

Pond

Nature Center Building

Parking
Trail Head

Self-Guiding
Nature Trail

Orchard Trail

Adventure
Trail

Observation
Tower

Prairie
Vista Trail

Road DT

General Hiking Trail

N
W — E
S

Brown's Fen Trail

Platform

Managed
Fen

Larger Fen

Elevated
Platform

Retzer Nature Center

Impoundment

Hillside Prairie Establishment Trail 👟 👟 👟 (0.4 mile
—blue markers) also varies in elevation, descending to a pond
at its lowest portion. It shows how the moisture of prairie soils,
as determined by elevation of the landscape, affects the kinds
of plant species that will grow. More than two decades of research at Retzer underscore the importance of choosing the
right species for prairie restoration.

Brown's Fen Trail 👟 👟 👟 (0.75 mile—brown
markers) travels around a fen, which is an alkaline wetland.
Boardwalks traverse wet portions of the trail and an elevated
platform overlooks the fen. The trail goes through woods, over
a dam, and along a farm field, providing opportunities to see
a variety of wildlife. Observers on the path have seen great
horned owls, several kinds of warblers, and woodcocks doing
their spring courtship dance.

General Hiking Trail 👟 👟 👟 (0.9 mile—green markers) forms a loop around the property delineating the original
bequest of the Retzers, who worked to restore their depleted
farm in the years before the Nature Center was established. It
passes through restored prairies, a hayfield managed to encourage grassland birds, old field, pine and cedar plantations, and
mixed woodlands.

Orchard Trail 👟 👟 👟 (0.3 mile—purple markers), a
spur from the General Hiking Trail, passes an old orchard and
leads to an observation tower overlooking a creek valley.

Degree of difficulty. Trails range in elevation from 1,020 feet
above sea level atop a drumlin to 845 feet at the dam near
Brown's Fen. With the exception of the Adventure Trail, which
has asphalt paving, trails are natural surface, with wood chips
covering damp and wooded areas. Retzer has built extensive
boardwalks on Brown's Fen Trail and the General Hiking Trail.
You'll find the usually wide footpaths to be well marked and
easy to follow.

How to get there. From Waukesha's west city limits go west on U.S. Highway 18 about 1.7 miles, then south on Road DT a short distance to the center's entrance.

Regulations. You may hike the trails any day between sunrise and 10:00 P.M. The nature center building is open daily from 8:00 A.M. to 4:30 P.M., except major holidays. Dogs and horses are prohibited, as are trail bicycles. Retzer urges hikers to stay on trails and to remove nothing, living or dead.

You may cross-country ski on a separate trail, which is periodically groomed.

Facilities. There are restrooms in the nature center building and parking nearby. The center has nature and bird identification displays, a small retail counter, meeting space, offices, and a laboratory.

Other points of interest in area

Also operated by Waukesha County, *Nashotah Park* has five hiking trails over terrain with pronounced glacial features. About halfway between Oconomowoc and Hartland on U.S. Highway 16, take County C north 0.5 mile to the park entrance on the left.

Dodge County

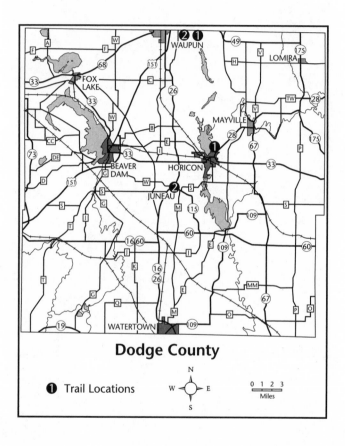

Dodge County

1 Trail Locations

N
W · E
S

0 1 2 3
Miles

1 Walk through a Wetland of International Importance

Horicon Marsh, near Horicon, Mayville, and Waupun

When I first entered this 31,904-acre preserve from the south on a trail around Quick's Point, I became immediately aware that I was in a very special place. It was not just because of the cacophony of hundreds of Canada geese preparing to take flight. Ducks hurried overhead to a destination unknown to me. Great egrets in the marsh posed majestically on their reedlike legs. A pair of elegant tundra swans plied the water in the background while courageous little tree swallows dove toward me to keep me away from their nests. In Horicon Marsh you don't just observe birds; you enter respectfully into their space. I tried to intrude as little as possible.

Called the Everglades of the North, Horicon Marsh has been declared a Wetland of International Importance by the Convention on Wetlands. It is divided by governmental jurisdiction into two parts. In the north the Horicon National Wildlife Refuge totals 20,976 acres. A straight east-west border divides it from the state-owned, 10,928-acre Horicon Marsh Wildlife Area. Each jurisdiction includes excellent walking trails.

Description and special features

North—National Wildlife Refuge

Egret Nature Trail. Each trail in the federal refuge provides a different wildlife viewing opportunity. Unique in this marsh, about half of this 0.4-mile trail consists of floating, 10-foot sections of boardwalk through open water and cattails. Although I didn't see any egrets during my walk there, I'm sure, with any luck, you could approach them closely if you could walk quietly enough. The trail begins and ends at a small parking lot off the Auto Tour Route.

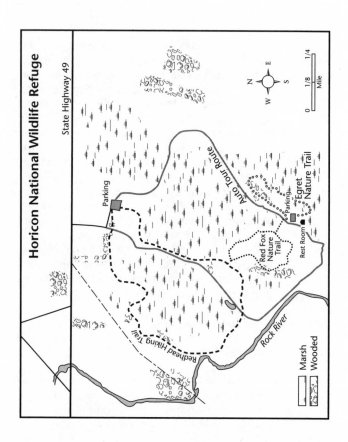

Horicon National Wildlife Refuge

State Highway 49

Auto Tour Route

Parking

Egret Nature Trail

Parking

Red Fox Nature Trail

Rest Room

Redhead Hiking Trail

Rock River

N
W E
S

0 1/8 1/4
Mile

Marsh
Wooded

Red Fox Nature Trail. From the same parking lot, this 0.5-mile trail loops mostly over a grassy meadow, where upland wildlife may be seen, and through a small stand of immature hardwoods. Of special interest are an old, high stone fence and a field-stone foundation along the trail, probably the remains of a barn on this former farmland. Sections of stone fence separate the upland from the marsh at several locations in the area of the trails. At its northernmost point the trail connects with the Redhead Hiking Trail. Surface is grass and some thin gravel.

Redhead Hiking Trail. This 2.5-mile trail begins at the main parking lot and loops around a large marsh, bordering it closely for good viewing of waterfowl. It closely passes the Rock River, which flows through Horicon Marsh. The surface is mostly natural turf.

Auto Tour Route. Opened in 1994, a 3.2-mile blacktop and gravel drive is open to hikers only during the days and hours it is closed to cars. Starting from the main parking lot, it generally follows the route of the Redhead Hiking Trail for about a mile, turns southeast along the bank of the Rock River, then turns northeast between marsh and prairie, and returns through a marsh to the parking lot. Informational stations along the way highlight nearby features of the marsh.

South—The State's Wildlife Area

Quick's Point Hiking Trail. Take your binoculars on this 1.5-mile trail. It provides the best opportunities to view birds and other wildlife in the marsh from a footpath. From a parking lot off Palmatory Street just north of Horicon the path loops around Quick's Point, where a DNR field office is located. Starting in a mostly oak forest, you will descend toward the edge of the marsh and a goose pond, where I observed numerous geese, ducks, and a few great egrets. The path enters another woods and then turns east, crossing the point to another portion of the marsh. You'll have more excellent chances to observe wildlife along the path where it returns to the trailhead.

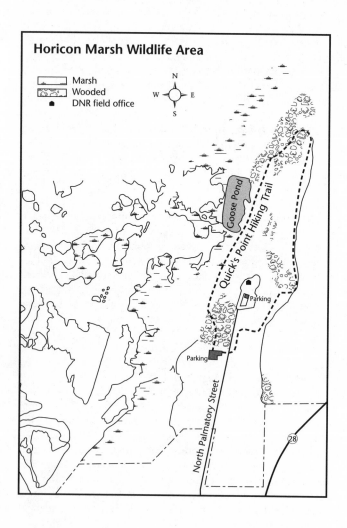

Horicon Marsh Wildlife Area

- Marsh
- Wooded
- DNR field office

Goose Pond

Quick's Point Hiking Trail

Parking

Parking

North Palmatory Street

28

Degree of difficulty. All the Horicon Marsh trails are wide and regularly maintained. Most slopes are gentle, and surfacing is natural turf with gravel or wood chips in a few places.

How to get there. Horicon National Wildlife Refuge trails are all located just south of State Highway 49, 2 miles east of Waupun. The Redhead Hiking Trail and the Auto Tour start from a main parking lot near the highway. The Egret and Red Fox nature trailheads are at a parking lot off the Auto Tour.

In the Horicon Marsh Wildlife Area, Quick's Point Hiking Trail starts from a parking lot on the west side of Palmatory Street 0.9 mile north of Horicon's East Lake Street.

Regulations. National Wildlife Refuge hiking trails are open from dawn to dusk, the year around. You may drive the Auto Tour Monday through Friday and some Saturdays from 8:00 A.M. to 3:00 P.M., April 15 through September 15. It is open for hiking all other times. No pets are allowed on any of the trails.

In the state's area, the Quick's Point Hiking Trail is open from dawn until 10:00 P.M. Dogs are not permitted on the trail. Elsewhere they must be under control at all times and leashed from April 15 through July 31 to avoid disturbing nesting birds.

Cross-country skiing is allowed in both the national and state areas, but trails are not groomed.

Facilities. Parking is available at all trails. In the federal refuge there is one pit toilet at the parking lot near the Egret and Red Fox nature trailheads. In the state area, pit toilets are located in the parking lot of the DNR field office north of the trail parking lot.

The Wisconsin DNR provides public naturalist programs on weekends during the spring and fall. The free programs are conducted at the Quick's Point field office. The state plans to develop a Horicon Marsh International Education Center. According to state wildlife educator William Volkert, it will be a world-class facility providing an array of interpretive exhibits, displays, and programs. Hiking trails will also be expanded.

Other points of interest in area

Built and sustained by volunteers, the *Marsh Haven Nature Center* provides a nature theater, wildlife art gallery, museum, and 1.5 miles of hiking trails. There is a small admission fee, or you may become a member, pay an annual fee, and use the center free of additional charge. Open from mid-April to early December, the center is located on the north side of State Highway 49 about 0.2 mile east of the federal refuge parking lot.

Boat tours and canoe rentals are available in Horicon at the *Blue Heron Landing*, on State Highway 33 at the Rock River Bridge. Either means of transportation will provide an opportunity to see marsh wildlife close up, including that in the *Four-mile Island Rookery*. This 15-acre island in the state wildlife area is the largest great blue heron and great egret rookery in Wisconsin. You may also see black-crowned night herons and double-crested cormorants. Mating and nesting activities take place from late March to May. To protect the birds, the island itself is closed to the public April 1–September 15.

2 A Tale of Two Counties

Wild Goose State Trail, between Juneau and Fond du Lac

To paraphrase Dickens, this is a tale of two counties. In 1985 the Chicago and Northwestern Railroad applied to abandon a corridor that included a 34-mile section between Juneau in Dodge County to the south and Fond du Lac in Fond du Lac County to the north. The two counties responded differently. The Fond du Lac County Board soon approved a pact with the state DNR, which had acquired most of the property, to fund the development of a multi-use trail.

Dodge County fathers, however, said no. Enter Juneau citizen Virginia Seaholm and a large group of sympathizers. After considerable lobbying, Seaholm's group convinced the Dodge County Board to reverse its decision, but with one important caveat: The citizens had to raise their own money to develop the trail. They formed the Friends of the Recreation Trail, which has since raised some $75,000 to provide paving, informational kiosks, signs, and so on. The group even publishes its own newsletter and sends it to more than 600 supporters.

Description and special features. From Fond du Lac the trail goes southwest through Oakfield to the Horicon Marsh. It curves south, bordering the marsh on the west. Users will enjoy the marsh's huge population of migrating and resident birds and other wildlife. Some 250 species of birds have been sighted. The trail passes through woodlots, prairie remnants, and farm fields, as well as the village of Burnett, on its way to State Highway 60 south of Juneau.

In the spring of 1995 the trail detoured three sections of land totaling 4.4 miles. Efforts were underway by the two counties to acquire two small sections near Oak Center and just north of the marsh as well as a larger section just north of Burnett.

Degree of difficulty. Limestone screenings provide a firm paving on this level railroad bed for easy biking or walking.

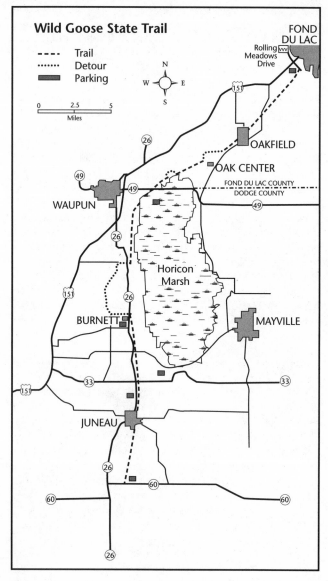

Wild Goose State Trail

- - - - Trail
.... Detour
▬ Parking

N
W · E
S

0   2.5   5
Miles

FOND DU LAC
Rolling Meadows Drive
151
26
49
OAKFIELD
OAK CENTER
FOND DU LAC COUNTY
DODGE COUNTY
49
WAUPUN
26
151
26
Horicon Marsh
BURNETT
MAYVILLE
33
151
33
JUNEAU
26
60
60
60
26

How to get there. In southwestern Fond du Lac, begin the trail from a parking lot on the south side of Rolling Meadows Drive 0.6 mile east of U.S. 151. In Juneau the entry point is accessed by going north from East Center Street 0.3 mile east of North Main Street (State Highway 26). You may also enter at road intersections along the way.

Regulations. In both counties the multi-use trail permits walkers, bicycles, wheelchairs, and cross-country skiers. From December 1 to March 31 snowmobiles are permitted when there is adequate snow cover. All-terrain vehicles are also permitted during those months, but only in Dodge County. Horses are not permitted on the limestone surface or any portion north of Juneau, but they may use a 3.5-mile section south from Juneau to State Highway 60. Dogs must be leashed.

Facilities. You may park at the trailhead in Fond du Lac, at the Rolling Meadows Golf Course just west of there, at the Marsh Haven Nature Center parking lot 0.25 mile east of the trail on State Highway 49, at the Horicon National Wildlife Refuge parking lot nearby, in the Burnett Fireman's Park 0.25 mile west of the trail in Burnett, at the Dodge County Airport north of Juneau, in Juneau City Park on Lincoln Street, or at the southern trailhead at State Highway 60.

There are restrooms at most of the parking locations.

A brochure, available at many nearby business establishments, provides more information. Copies are also available from the Dodge County Planning and Development Department (414-386-3705) and the Fond du Lac County Planning and Parks Department (414-929-3135). Send contributions to the Friends of the Recreation Trail, P.O. Box 72, Juneau, WI 53039.

Other points of interest in area

Federal and state agencies manage the 31,000-acre *Horicon Marsh.* In the north, the Horicon National Wildlife Refuge and, in the south, the DNR's Horicon Marsh Wildlife Area provide opportunities for hiking, wildlife watching, canoeing, fishing, hunting, and winter sports (see pp. 180–86).

North Central

. . . At daybreak I am the sole owner of all the acres I can walk over. It is not only boundaries that disappear, but also the thought of being bounded.

Aldo Leopold, A SAND COUNTY ALMANAC

1. Portage County
2. Waupaca County
3. Wood County

Portage County

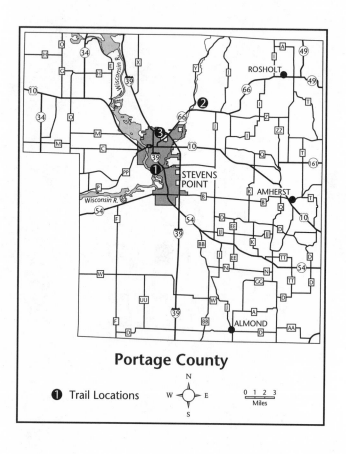

Portage County

❶ Trail Locations

N
W ⬥ E
S

0 1 2 3
Miles

1 Award-Winning Trail Circles City and Suburbs

Green Circle, Stevens Point

A cynic once said a camel is a horse put together by a committee. No cynics were involved when Stevens Point and four surrounding communities, Portage County, more than 20 corporate and individual private land owners, a university, the Wisconsin Department of Natural Resources, and several public utilities worked together to plan and build this trail. Their cooperative effort earned an award from the National Park Service for the 24-mile Green Circle.

Description and special features. Because of its length and diversity, the Green Circle is hard to characterize. The trail follows the banks of two rivers, the Wisconsin and the Plover. It goes over prairies, through a nature preserve, across streams and railroad tracks, through numerous parks, and even through the property of a paper mill.

Surfacing ranges from asphalt to granite gravel and wood chips. Twelve connected segments, each with its own individual identity, make up the trail.

Roy Menzel, a retired public relations executive, is a member of the Green Circle Committee, the prime movers for the trail. He pointed to major segments along the banks of the two rivers as trail highlights. For example, the River Pines segment, accessed from the west end of Sherman Avenue, follows the Wisconsin River through a pristine white and red pine forest past historic Echo Dells.

Degree of difficulty. The trail is wide, paved, and well maintained. Most of its route is over level terrain. Several sturdy bridges span streams. Although bicyclists also use the trail, an effort is made to enforce a 15-mile-per-hour speed limit and trail-sharing rules.

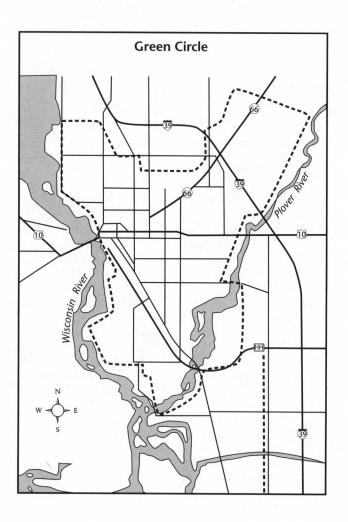

Green Circle

How to get there. You may enter the trail from many points in the Greater Stevens Point area. There are nine designated parking lots on the circle, or you may park on most residential streets.

Regulations. No motorized vehicles are permitted. Dogs must be leashed. Bikes are permitted except on several segments where signs indicate alternate routes on streets. The trail is open 24 hours a day except in parks where there are restricted hours.

Facilities. Trail builders have provided benches on some segments. Restrooms are available in several parks the trail traverses.

Other points of interest in area

Part of the trail is in the Schmeeckle Reserve. Its Visitor Center includes the *Wisconsin Conservation Hall of Fame,* honoring the contributions of Aldo Leopold, John Muir, Sigurd Olsen, and others. See page 203 for open hours.

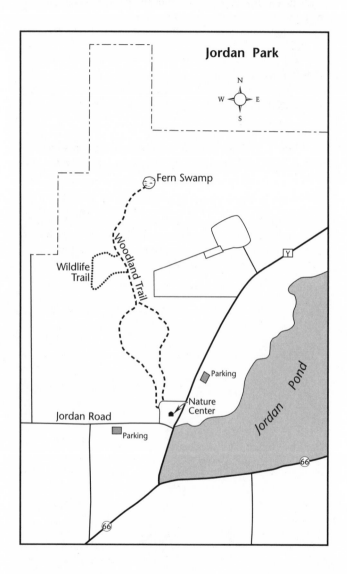

Jordan Park

N
W   E
S

Fern Swamp

Woodland Trail

Wildlife
Trail

Y

Parking

Nature
Center

Jordan Road

Parking

Jordan Pond

66

66

2 Take a Path through Old-Growth Pines

Jordan Park, northeast of Stevens Point

Not far from the Plover River a county park contains giant white pines that were too immature to cut when the area was logged in the mid-nineteenth century. Those giant trees and the red maples that grow under them now form a subclimax forest through which a trail loops.

Description and special features. The **Woodland Trail,** a nature trail with 25 informational stops, goes among the pines, maples, a few hemlocks, and other trees. Be sure to pick up the well-written guide available at a dispenser at the trailhead. It explains how the subclimax forest came to be and its place in the order of forest succession.

In contrast, a second loop, the **Wildlife Trail,** goes through a part of the forest in which the older trees were cut in 1966. Such first-stage trees as aspen, oak, and balsam have established themselves here.

Take the main trail to its end to reach Fern Swamp, where, according to the guide, nine species of ferns grow.

Degree of difficulty. All trails are wide, on level terrain, and have a natural surface. Fern Swamp may be muddy in wet weather.

How to get there. From U.S. 51 in northeast Stevens Point, take State Highway 66 northeast for 3.1 miles to County Y on the left. The park is on both sides of County Y just north of 66.

Regulations. The park is open to day users from 6:00 A.M. to 11:00 P.M. Pets must be leashed. No bikes are allowed on trails. Cross-country skiing is permitted.

Facilities. The 271-acre park includes an 85-acre pond and swimming beach, restrooms, a picnic area and shelter, and a ball field. There is also a 22-site campground. Park either in the

lot on the east side of County Y or in the lot on the south side
of Jordan Road.

Other points of interest in area

The *Nature Center* in the park has programs about nature
and wildlife. The center is open weekends from Memorial Day
through Labor Day. For information on current programs and
hours, call the county parks office: 715-346-1433.

Also operated by the county, *Lake Emily Park* near Amherst
Junction has a nature trail going over a terminal moraine. The
park contains many effigy mounds built by the Woodland Indians between 700 and 1,300 years ago.

3 Trails Lace Stevens Point Natural Area

Schmeeckle Reserve, Stevens Point

Through the efforts of Fred J. Schmeeckle, the University of Wisconsin–Stevens Point was first in the nation to offer conservation as a major. The natural area named for him preserves forest, wetland, and prairie. Trails and boardwalks provide opportunities to get close to them.

Description and special features. You can view the 207-acre reserve's assets from three major trails and interconnecting spurs and condition yourself on a fitness trail as well.

Lake Trail goes through mostly conifer woodland for about a mile around Lake Joanis, a serene pond with a forested island in the middle. This trail is also part of Stevens Point's Green Circle (see pp. 194–97).

Reflections Trail, which loops from the Visitor Center and back, was designed for leisurely walking. Allow at least 20 minutes to read the interpretive quotes on stations along the way. Children and adults will enjoy the swing and treehouse constructed by the reserve.

Granite Trail is a mile-long abandoned road through forest and prairie. You can view reserve wetlands but keep your feet dry on the sturdy bridges or boardwalks along a trail that connects Granite Trail and Lake Trail.

The 19-station *Fitness Trail* winds through a meadow and cattail marsh in the southern part of the reserve. You can also view wildlife from an observation tower there.

Degree of difficulty. Trail surfaces include wood chips, crushed rock, and the above-mentioned boardwalks. There are also unsurfaced portions. The reserve maintains its trails well over mostly level terrain.

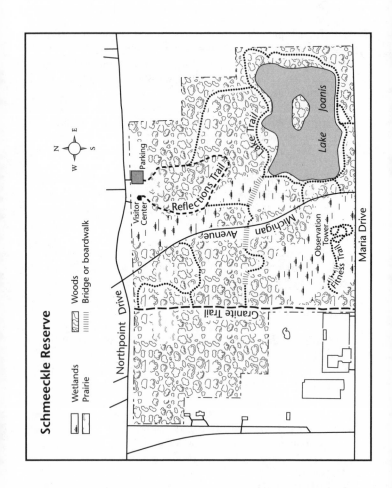

Schmeeckle Reserve

Wetlands
Prairie
Woods
Bridge or boardwalk

N
W E
S

Northpoint Drive

Visitor Center
Parking

Reflections Trail

Lake Trail

Michigan Avenue

Granite Trail

Observation Tower

Fitness Trail

Lake Joanis

Maria Drive

How to get there. The Visitor Center with its Wisconsin Conservation Hall of Fame and a demonstration area about composting are located near the northeast corner of Schmeeckle Reserve on Northpoint Drive just east of Michigan Avenue. You can enter Granite Trail and Fitness Trail from Maria Drive west of Michigan Avenue or Lake Trail east of Michigan Avenue, which runs generally north-south through the reserve.

Regulations. Use trails only during daylight hours. The Visitor Center opens Monday–Friday at 8:00 A.M., Saturday at 10:00 A.M., and Sunday at noon. It closes each day at 5:00 P.M. No pets or collecting are allowed. Biking is permitted "at slow speeds" on the Lake Trail and Granite Trail. Walkers have the right-of-way. The reserve allows cross-country skiing but does not groom trails.

Facilities. You may park at the Visitor Center and use its restrooms during open hours. There is also parking along Maria Drive and a restroom near the trailheads of Granite Trail and Fitness Trail.

Other points of interest in area

In downtown Stevens Point over 60 buildings compose the *Mathias Mitchell Public Square,* the Main Street Historic District. A guidebook is available in stores or at the Visitors Bureau at 23 Park Ridge Drive. Phone 800-236-4636.

The Visitors Bureau can also provide a pamphlet, *Wildlife Watching in the Stevens Point–Amherst Area,* with five auto or bike tours. It promises viewing of eagle and osprey nests, bluebird trails, duck-feeding areas, country roads, and rivers.

Waupaca County

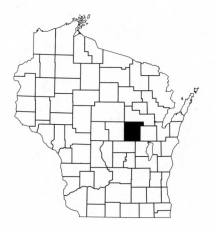

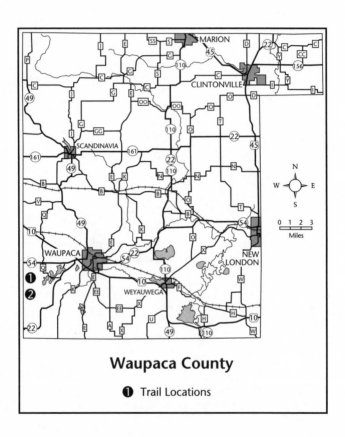

Waupaca County

❶ Trail Locations

1 Lakes and Moraine Highlight State Park's Trails

Hartman Creek State Park, west of Waupaca

Located on the upper lakes of the famed Waupaca Chain O'Lakes, Hartman Creek State Park has trails around lakes, on a dike, through an old orchard, and over a glacial moraine. Among its 14 miles of trails is a segment of the Ice Age National Scenic Trail. In addition to the usual state park activities— camping, swimming, picnicking, and so on—you can also see a butterfly garden or borrow a book from the park's lending library.

Description and special features.

Dike Hiking Trail. Paved with limestone screenings, this unique 1-mile trail runs atop a dike separating Hartman Lake from a creek channeled alongside it, then loops back. I saw nine species of wildflowers during my June walk. Park naturalist Lea Bousley says yarrow, bindweed, bittersweet nightshade, goatsbeard, spiderwort, bedstraw, and buttercups grow there.

John Schmelling Fitness Trail. A red pine plantation will be your gymnasium for doing push-ups and other exercises at stations on this short trail. It's located on the south side of Hartman Lake.

Deer Path Trail. This sometimes narrow and mostly unsurfaced path goes through a forest of pines and hardwoods for 1 mile around Allen Lake. Thick lakeside undergrowth includes a large plot of club moss. In the lake I saw two huge snapping turtles apparently vying for territory. Painted turtles and the rare Blanding's turtle also inhabit the lakes, says park superintendent Merle Lang.

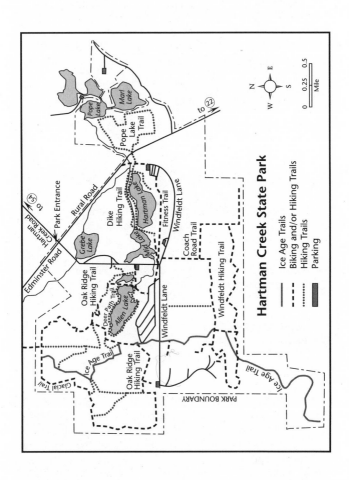

Hartman Creek State Park

Ice Age Trails
Biking and/or Hiking Trails
Hiking Trails
Parking

0   0.25   0.5
Mile

N
W   E
S

Pope Lake Trail. 👟 👟 About 1.5 miles, this trail through forest and meadow follows a loop from Hartman Lake to Pope and Marl lakes and back.

Windfeldt Hiking Trail. 👟 👟 👟 Going through an old orchard and up one of the highest hills in the park, this 1.5-mile trail provides excellent opportunities to observe bluebirds and bobolinks, according to park literature.

Coach Road Trail. 👟 👟 Part of an old stage coach route between Oshkosh and Stevens Point, this 0.85-mile trail is popular among bikers. A new trail feature is a wildlife observation blind for viewing fauna in a wetland habitat. The trail connects to the Windfeldt Hiking Trail.

Oak Ridge Hiking Trail. 👟 👟 👟 A variety of interconnecting routes lace the rolling topography of the moraine in the northwest part of the park. A former farm, the area has meadow and woodland of hardwoods with some pines. Hikers will pass a deep glacial kettle along the ***Glacial Trail,*** a small section of the Oak Ridge Hiking Trail. There is also a room-sized glacial erratic on the trail. Total distance is about 5 miles.

Ice Age National Scenic Trail. See the separate trail account on pages 211–13 for details.

Degree of difficulty. Trail difficulty is as varied as the terrain in the park. Most trails are well maintained but have a natural surface. The lakeside Deer Path Trail goes very close in a few places to a steep lakeside bank, which is not fenced off. The Oak Ridge Hiking Trail goes over the typically hummocky glacial moraine in the northwest part of the park. Watch for trail bikes, which are permitted on the Coach Road and Windfeldt trails and a portion of the Oak Ridge Hiking Trail.

How to get there. From State Highway 54 about 5 miles west of Waupaca, take Hartman Creek Road south 1.5 miles to the park.

Regulations. Day-use hours are 6:00 A.M. to 11:00 P.M. Pets must be leashed. Off-road biking is permitted only where signs indicate. A state park annual or daily permit is required.

Facilities. Hartman Creek has all the facilities of a full-service state park including restrooms, camp sites, picnic shelters, and swimming beach. Fishing is very popular in the many lakes of the park.

Other points of interest in area

In 26-acre *Oakwood Park* a walkway of railroad ties on the nature trail provides access to a small wilderness pond. This Waupaca County park also has picnic tables and grills, playground equipment, restroom facilities, drinking water, and a boat launch. It's located on County Q 1 mile west of State Highway 22 among the Chain O'Lakes southwest of Waupaca.

2 Trail Follows Terminal Moraine of Green Bay Glacier Lobe

Ice Age National Scenic Trail, Waupaca-Portage Counties Segment

When the Laurentide Ice Sheet pushed into Wisconsin, the Green Bay lobe reached its farthest extension about 15,000 years ago and formed a terminal moraine along what is now the Portage-Waupaca county line. A segment of the Ice Age National Scenic Trail there shows off such glacial features as erratics, drumlins, and a kettle.

Description and special features. About 15 miles in length running generally north-south, the trail begins in the south at Second Avenue in Portage County. Going north, the trail enters Emmons Creek Fish and Wildlife Area and forms the large Faraway Valley Loop, named for a farm that once occupied the area. The trail goes over open fields and crosses Emmons Creek twice, once by footbridge and once over a road bridge.

Continuing north through woodlands of hardwoods and some pines, the trail crosses Stratton Lake Road and Emmons Creek Road before entering Hartman Creek State Park. The rare blue karner butterfly, a protected species, frequents patches of wild lupine along southern portions of the trail. To protect the butterfly, the park doesn't reveal specific locations, says park superintendent Merle Lang.

The trail goes over pronounced moraine topography in the northwest part of the state park, passing a giant erratic, a boulder that was transported by the glacier from somewhere much farther north. Hikers will also pass a deep kettle near the northwest corner of the park.

Leaving the park in the north, the trail traverses private land, going over a maple-covered drumlin and crossing Allen Creek on a small bridge. Continuing north to State Highway 54, the trail goes near Turner's Farm Market, operated by a member of the same family that owned the farm in Faraway Valley, according to Lang.

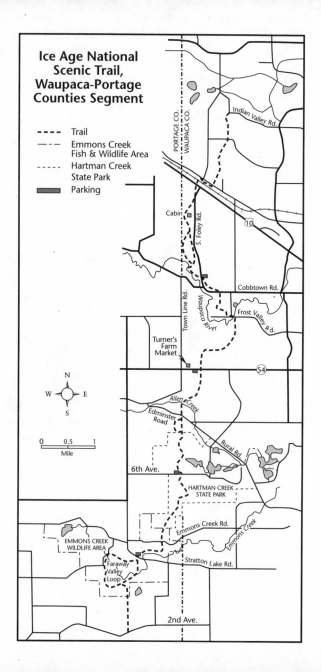

Ice Age National Scenic Trail, Waupaca-Portage Counties Segment

- – – – Trail
- – ·· – Emmons Creek Fish & Wildlife Area
- – – – Hartman Creek State Park
- ▬ Parking

PORTAGE CO.
WAUPACA CO.

Indian Valley Rd.

10

Cabin

S. Foley Rd.

Cobbtown Rd.

Frost Valley Rd.

Town Line Rd.

Waupaca River

Turner's Farm Market

54

N
W · E
S

0   0.5   1
Mile

Allen Creek

Edminster Road

Rural Rd.

6th Ave.

HARTMAN CREEK STATE PARK

EMMONS CREEK WILDLIFE AREA

Emmons Creek Rd.

Emmons Creek

Faraway Valley Loop

Stratton Lake Rd.

2nd Ave.

After crossing the Waupaca River on a bridge of Frost Valley Road and continuing north, the trail is split into a loop. Blue blazes mark the trail along South Foley Road so a hiker can park, walk a loop, and return to his or her car without doubling back on the trail. A portion of the loop follows the bank of the river, offering scenic views of it.

Just south of U.S. Highway 10, a rustic cabin with pit toilet but no water can be used by hikers on a first-come, first-served basis. From a hill north of the cabin, hikers can view a drumlin and outwash valley to the north.

After crossing U.S. 10, the trail returns to the rolling moraine. The trail ends at Indian Valley Road.

Degree of difficulty. The 15-mile segment goes over a variety of terrain, with some steep slopes on the terminal moraine. As with most portions of the Ice Age Trail, it is designed for back-country hiking and receives little regular maintenance outside the state park. Yellow blazes and signs mark the main trail. Blue blazes indicate the scenic loop; and green blazes, the Faraway Valley Loop.

How to get there. The trail runs generally along the Portage and Waupaca county line, starting in Portage County at Second Avenue. It crosses the county boundary line several times in the state park, and continues north in Waupaca County to its end. Park in one of the lots listed below.

Regulations. Stay on the trail where it traverses private land. No bicycles are allowed. Cross-country skiing is permitted, but the trail is not groomed. Hikers are urged to wear hunter's orange in the Emmons Creek Fish and Wildlife Area and on private land during the fall and winter hunting seasons.

Facilities. There are small parking lots at Stratton Lake Road, about 400 feet west of the trail on Windfeldt Lane in the state park, at State Highway 54, and on Foley Road 0.25 mile north of Cobbtown Road. The state park has restrooms and drinking water. There is also a pit toilet at the cabin south of U.S. 10.

Wood County

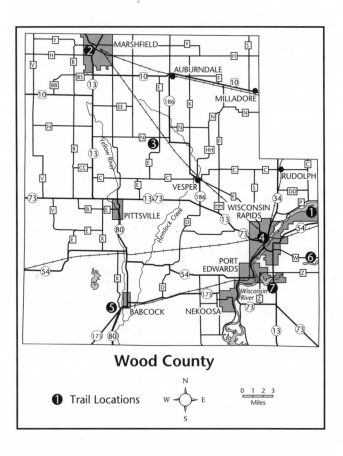

Wood County

① Trail Locations

N W—✦—E S

0 1 2 3
Miles

1 Self-Guiding Trail Shows How Managed Forest Grows

Consolidated Papers Forest Tour II, Biron

A manufacturer of paper for printing, Consolidated Papers, Inc., owns 310,000 acres of forest lands in Wisconsin. A self-guiding trail through a 110-acre stand of conifers and hardwoods provides information about tree growth, harvesting, and other aspects of forest management.

Description and special features. The 1.5-mile trail loops through the forest and atop a dike bordering a cranberry bog. Available in a metal box at the trailhead, a printed guide is keyed to 26 numbered posts along the way. Rather than concentrating on tree identification, the guide tells about the history of the trees and how they thrive (or not) under various forest living conditions.

Degree of difficulty. While mostly on level ground, the trail is bumpy with surface roots in places. It tends to be narrow, especially along the top of the dike, and damp in low spots. Mosquitoes are especially abundant in this lowland forest. Bring repellent.

How to get there. You'll find the trailhead parking lot on the south side of County U (North Biron Drive) in Biron 0.5 mile east of Forty-eighth Street and 0.5 mile west of Sixty-fourth Street.

Regulations. No motor vehicles are allowed on the trail, which is open daily from sunrise to sunset. You may cross-country ski.

Facilities. Parking.

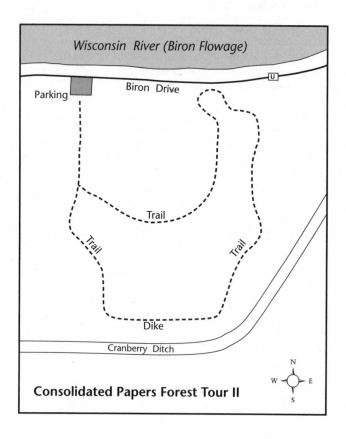

Wisconsin River (Biron Flowage)

Parking

Biron Drive

U

Trail

Trail

Trail

Dike

Cranberry Ditch

N
W   E
S

Consolidated Papers Forest Tour II

Other points of interest in area

Directly across the street from the parking lot, Biron Flowage of the Wisconsin River offers boating and fishing. Consolidated Papers, Inc., provides a boat launch nearby. Just east of the forest on Sixty-fourth Street you may drive through operating cranberry bogs.

2 Visit City's History on Walking Tour

Downtown Marshfield Historical Tour

Surrounded by hardwood forests and patches of pine, early Marshfield was predestined to be a lumber town. The railroad came and then the first sawmill, drawing workers and related businesses by the hundreds. But a 1887 fire destroyed 250 homes and small businesses. Determined to continue, businessmen rebuilt with fire-resistant brick and mortar. Many of those buildings remain today. Following a brochure available from the Visitors and Promotion Bureau, you can tour Marshfield's Downtown Historic District and view more than two dozen buildings that have been restored or preserved.

Description and special features. The tour covers about 6 blocks, with buildings on both sides of Central Avenue and several side streets. The brochure gives a brief history and architectural details of each building.

Degree of difficulty. You'll be walking wide, level, downtown sidewalks. The only possible hazard is the traffic at crosswalks, especially on Central Avenue.

How to get there. Marshfield is in northwest Wood County. Write for the brochure or stop by Marshfield Visitors and Promotion Bureau, 700 South Central Avenue, P.O. Box 868, Marshfield, WI 54449.

Regulations. None.

Facilities. Parking is available on surrounding streets.

Other points of interest in area

For a more rustic walking experience, *McMillan Wildlife Management Area* lies immediately north and northwest of the city. Over 1,000 acres of marshes, ponds, and lowland forests contain myriad wildlife. You can get into the area via access roads from north, south, east, or west. Service roads along dikes provide the best and driest hiking. Upon checking four different access roads, I found the best to be Marsh Road from the east. Take State Highway 97 northeast out of Marshfield to County E near the north city limits. Go north 3 miles to Marsh Road, then west about 1 mile to a parking lot.

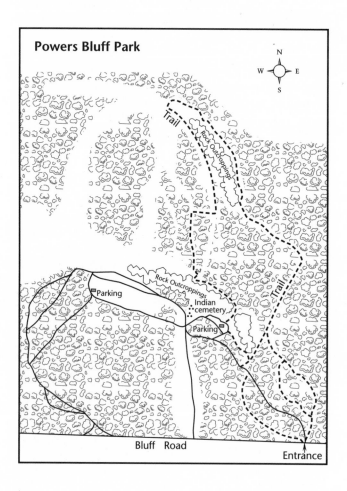

Powers Bluff Park

N
W · E
S

Trail

Rock Outcroppings

Rock Outcroppings

Parking

Indian cemetery

Parking

Trail

Bluff Road

Entrance

3 Rocky Nature Trail Loops through Scientific Area

Powers Bluff Park, Arpin

Powers Bluff, the tallest hill in Wood County, is a "monadnock," an ancient worn-down mountain composed entirely of quartzite. In the 160-acre county park on the hill, the self-guiding Potawatomi Nature Trail takes the hiker through a designated scientific preservation area. A printed guide identifies 50 species of trees and shrubs that are part of the hill's diverse ecology.

Description and special features. The trail loops from the top of the bluff partway down the east side and back up to the entrance road, about 200 yards from the trailhead. Arrows mounted on posts show the way through some thick woods and around quartzite outcroppings. Allow about 2 hours to hike the entire trail if you stop at all the guideposts. The printed guides may or may not be available at the trailhead. The county parks department will mail you one in advance of your hike if you call 715-421-8422. Maple trees make up most of the hillside forest. You'll especially enjoy the colors of an autumn walk.

Degree of difficulty. The path is sometimes narrow, frequently rocky, and occasionally steep. While most of it is unsurfaced, some portions have been graveled.

How to get there. From where County Highways N and E cross on the west side of Arpin, take E south 1 mile to Bluff Road, then west 1 mile to the park entrance on the right.

Regulations. The park is open for hiking May 1–October 31 from 8:00 A.M. to 10:00 P.M. Pets must be leashed. Cross-country skiing is permitted from 10:00 A.M. to 5:00 P.M. and the trail is groomed.

Facilities. As well as parking, there are picnic tables, play-ground equipment, and pit toilets. Somewhat of a mecca for winter sports enthusiasts, Powers Bluff offers cross-country and down-hill skiing and snow tubing. Two rope tows return both skiers and tubers to the start of the 250-foot descent. There is also a shelter house, with a drinking fountain on the outside.

Other points of interest in area

You can hike the cross-country ski trails of two other county parks in the area. Mowed trails meander over 1,000 acres for summer use in *Dexter Park*, 6 miles south of Pittsville at the junction of State Highways 80 and 54. For wilderness hiking, try the unmowed ski trails of *Richfield Recreation Area*, on County A, 1 mile north of its junction with N.

4 Riverside Trail Is a Walk in the Park

Wisconsin River Walk, Wisconsin Rapids

A river runs through it, and Wisconsin Rapids' history and geography have been shaped by that river—the Wisconsin. Fittingly, the city built a scenic walking and biking trail along its banks.

Description and special features. Routed through Lyons and Ben Hanson parks and across the riverside property of the State Office Building, the 1.1-mile trail is literally a walk in the park. Mature pines and younger maples tower overhead as you follow the path over mowed and groomed park land. The silent-running river dominates your view. The scenery attracts strollers as well as brisk walkers and joggers. Although bikes are allowed, I saw none during my visit.

Degree of difficulty. It's an easy stroll on a completely level, asphalt path.

How to get there. The path runs along the northwest side of the Wisconsin River from Riverview Expressway to Boles Creek. You may park in Lyons Park at the northeast end or in Ben Hanson Park, near the boat ramp, at the southwest end. South Second Avenue borders both parks.

Regulations. The parks are open from 5:00 A.M. to 11:00 P.M. No dogs or motor vehicles are allowed.

Facilities. Each park has restrooms, playground equipment, picnic tables, and parking. There are benches along the trail.

Other points of interest in area

Several miles south in Port Edwards, the *Alexander House Art and History Center* houses the extensive historical archives of the Nekoosa Edwards Paper Company, including photos, books, documents, and letters. A permanent art collection and frequent traveling exhibits include local as well as nationally known artists. The center is located at 1131 Wisconsin River Drive. No admission is charged. For current hours, call 715-887-3442.

5 Driving and Hiking Trails Access Wildlife Viewing

Sandhill Wildlife Area, Babcock

Original settlers found fertile marshes and forested uplands in this part of central Wisconsin, but several stages of destruction followed. They harvested the trees and left the uplands barren. Farmers used steam-powered dredges to ditch and drain marshes, but the soil proved to be too acidic for growing crops. Some kinds of wildlife were hunted to near extinction.

The exhausted land's recovery began when Wallace Grange purchased 9,460 acres in the 1930s, enclosed it, and nurtured it while running a game farm. In 1962 the state bought it for use as a wildlife demonstration area. Today the Sandhill Wildlife Area serves as a living laboratory to test wildlife management techniques. Animals thrive in the marshes and woodlands. A visitor may see deer, ruffed grouse, owls, loons, eagles, geese, hares, and more. Even buffalo inhabit a portion of the preserve.

Staffers have built both driving and hiking trails to help visitors observe wildlife and learn how the land is managed to encourage growth and diversity.

Description and special features. To experience Sandhill thoroughly, take both the driving and the hiking trails.

Trumpeter Trail, a 14-mile auto trail, was designed to show as many facets of the wildlife area as possible: wetland, forest, and a quartzite bluff that protrudes 200 feet above the flatlands. Obtain a copy of the trail's interpretive guide at the gated trailhead near the headquarters and stop at each numbered post.

Swamp Buck Trail, a 3.5-mile hiking trail, goes across meadows, through woods, and over wetlands. You'll experience sedge marshes and forest communities of lowland alder or aspen and upland oak. The trail ends at stone-and-mortar stairs leading to the top of the North Bluff. The hiking trail begins at a parking lot on the Trumpeter Trail about a mile from the latter's

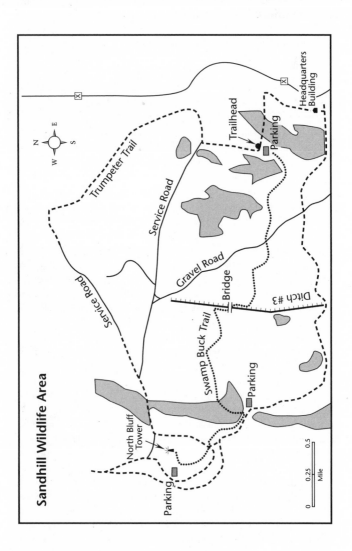

Sandhill Wildlife Area

Trumpeter Trail

Service Road

Service Road

Gravel Road

Swamp Buck Trail

Bridge

Ditch #3

Parking

Parking

Trailhead

Parking

Headquarters Building

North Bluff Tower

N

E

S

W

0   0.25   0.5

Mile

trailhead. If you're short of time but would like to hike a portion of the trail, park at a second lot less than a mile southeast of the bluff. If you want only to climb the bluff, drive to station 8 on Trumpeter Trail, where the stairs begin off a small parking lot.

Degree of difficulty. The trail is wide with a natural surface. Portions go over an old service road and well-worn deer trails. Terrain is mostly flat or gently sloping. Builders constructed boardwalks over wetlands and a bridge over Ditch #3, which contains open water. The three-shoe difficulty rating for this trail does not include the stairs, which climb directly and steeply up North Bluff. Management cautions that stairs and boardwalks may be slippery when wet.

How to get there. Just southwest of Babcock on State Highways 80 and 173, take County X north 0.7 mile to Sandhill's entrance on the left.

Regulations. Motor vehicles, dirt bikes, and horses are prohibited on Swamp Buck Trail. Dogs must be leashed. All items packed in should be packed out. Hikers are encouraged to take water and insect repellent. The gate at the Trumpeter trailhead is unlocked from sunrise to sunset from April (if the weather is not too wet) to the last week in October. Cross-country skiers may use a network of 11 miles of trails. Sandhill is closed to hikers and autos during the firearm deer hunting season.

Facilities. Parking, pit toilets, observation tower, rifle range.

Other points of interest in area

Adjacent to the southern border of Sandhill Wildlife Area, *Wood County Wildlife Area* and *Wood County Forest land* cover more than 21,000 acres. Their history and geography are similar to Sandhill's. Lying within the bed of old Glacial Lake Wisconsin, the soils are sandy or peaty. After failed farming efforts, the land reverted to the county and is now managed by the DNR to enhance wildlife resources. Wildlife areas are open to hunters, bird watchers, hikers, berry pickers, campers, and others. Hike along access roads and unmarked wilderness trails. You'll find them south of County Highway X and west of State Highway 173.

6 New Paved Trail Follows Park Land around Lake

South Wood County Park–Lake Wazeecha, Wisconsin Rapids

Since Wood County owns all but six parcels of land bordering Lake Wazeecha, the idea to build a hiking and biking path all the way around the long, placid lake had a lot of appeal. Builders completed the path in 1995, and it's been one of the county's most popular ever since.

Description and special features. Wooded park land surrounds Lake Wazeecha, so the environment of conifers and some hardwoods, over the gently undulating lakeside terrain, provides a refreshingly pleasant walk. On the north side of the lake, steel bridges cross two lagoon inlets. Where North Park Road comes close to the lake, the trail runs alongside the road for a short distance. On the lake's south side, the trail meanders through pine plantations and borders a large campground. A long footbridge on the park's east side runs along the dam that forms the lake.

Degree of difficulty. Compacted gravel paves most of the 4.1-mile trail. Slopes are short and gentle.

How to get there. From the east limits of Wisconsin Rapids, take County W (Lake Avenue) 2.6 miles southeast to North Park Road, which borders park land along the north side of the lake.

Regulations. The park land around the lake is open from 8:00 A.M. to 10:00 P.M. Park facilities are open from May 1 to October 31, although camping extends to November 30. No motor vehicles are allowed on the trail. Pets must be leashed.

Facilities. The parks provide restrooms, playgrounds, picnic shelters, well water, a swimming beach, and a bathhouse. There are parking lots on both the north and south sides of the lake.

South Wood County Park, on the south side, has extensive camping facilities. For reservations phone 715-421-8422.

Other points of interest in area

Nepco Lake County Park, just south of Wisconsin Rapids off U.S. Highway 13, has a 1.5-mile cross-country ski trail that is mowed for hiking when there is no snow. This day-use park also offers swimming and picnicking.

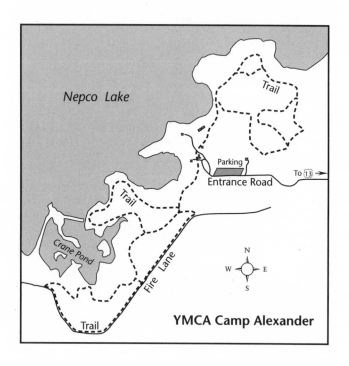

Nepco Lake

Trail

Parking

To ⑬ →

Entrance Road

Trail

Crane Pond

Fire Lane

N
W · E
S

Trail

YMCA Camp Alexander

7 Lakeside Views Highlight YMCA Trails

YMCA Camp Alexander, Wisconsin Rapids

Trail builders at Camp Alexander took full advantage of the camp's location on the shore of Lake Nepco for their hiking, biking, and cross-country ski trails. The trails follow the ups and downs of the hilly terrain and offer great lake views from some of the higher spots.

Description and special features. Between 4 and 5 miles of trails wind through the 300-acre camp. The original trails, with the best lake views, were designed for hiking. More have been built recently for hiking, biking, and cross-country skiing. The result is a varied network with lots of loops, going to the camp's farthest reaches through a forest of predominantly conifers with some hardwoods mixed in.

Degree of difficulty. At this writing, trails were all a natural surface of mowed grass or sandy earth. Wood chips may be added later, according to camp director Andy Boettcher. Trails are generally wide. Much of the trail network is on level ground. Hilly portions have short slopes, some of which are quite steep.

How to get there. From County Highway Z (Griffith Road) at Wisconsin Rapid's south city limit, take U.S. Highway 13 south 1 mile to Townline Road. Across from Townline, turn right onto the camp's entrance road.

Regulations. No motor vehicles are allowed. Dogs must be leashed in summer and are not allowed during the cross-country skiing season. While, officially, the trails are open only to YMCA members and their guests, "we allow the public to come in and use the trail," says Boettcher.

Facilities. The camp has restrooms in summer and pit toilets or portable units in winter. There is a separate parking lot on the entrance road for trail users.

Other points of interest in area

South Wood County Historical Museum houses exhibits dating from 1852 to the present. Located in a mansion built in 1907, the museum showcases the cranberry industry and Native American culture. It has old schoolrooms and an early 1900s general store. Kids will especially enjoy a children's toy room exhibiting old dolls and furniture. Open Sundays and Tuesdays from 1:00 P.M. to 4:00 P.M., the museum is located at 540 Third Street South in Wisconsin Rapids. Admission is free.

South Central

My earliest recollections of the country were gained on short walks with my grandfather when I was perhaps not over three years old.

John Muir, *The Story of My Boyhood and Youth*

1. Adams County
2. Juneau County
3. Marquette County
4. Waushara County

Adams County

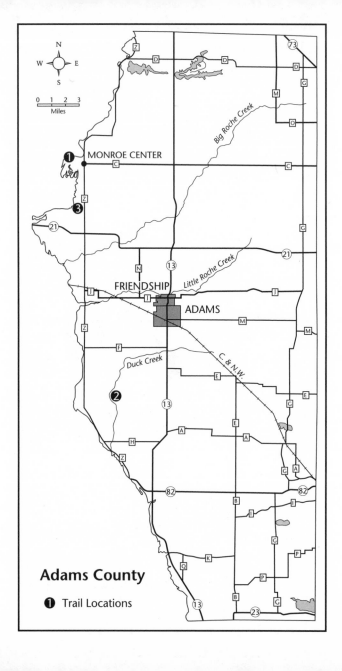

Adams County

1 Trail Locations

1 Fully Equipped County Park Offers Hiking and Much More

Petenwell County Park, Monroe Center

You'll enjoy hiking the trails at this especially well-equipped county park. And the lakeside park also has camp-sites (modern and primitive), a swimming beach, picnic tables and shelters, children's play areas, a boat launch, and a game room.

Description and special features. Two trails go south of the developed park. A wheelchair-accessible trail, with a com-pacted, crushed limestone surface, loops south from a trail-head parking lot and back north to Bighorn Avenue. A second hiking trail goes past primitive lakeside campsites, deep into the mixed conifer and deciduous woods, and onto a peninsula jutting into the Petenwell Flowage.

Degree of difficulty. Trails are on mostly level or gently sloping terrain. Some southern portions may be muddy in wet weather. As mentioned above, the wheelchair-accessible trail is paved. The hiking trail has mostly a natural surface, with wood chips in a few places.

How to get there. From the junction of County Highways C and Z in Monroe Center, go north on Z for 0.5 mile to Bighorn Avenue, then west for 0.9 mile to the trailhead parking lot on the left.

Regulations. The park is open for day users from 7:00 A.M. to 10:30 P.M. Park facilities open April 15 and close November 30. Trails are open the year around for hiking or cross-country ski-ing. Dogs must be leashed. Vehicles require a $2 permit, avail-able at the park.

Facilities. In addition to the park facilities mentioned above, there is a parking lot on Twentieth Drive near the primitive campsites. Restrooms and drinking water are available in the park.

Other points of interest in area

Camping, swimming, and picnicking are also available at *Castle Rock County Park,* on the Petenwell Flowage 7 miles west of Friendship, just south of the junction of County Highways Z and F.

2 Experience Wilderness Hiking at The Nature Conservancy's Big Preserve

Quincy Bluff and Wetlands Preserve, southeast of Adams

In 1990 the Wisconsin chapter of The Nature Conservancy acquired the first 1,400 acres of what has become one of its largest preserves. In cooperation with the DNR and private land owners, more than 3,300 acres were protected at this writing. The DNR planned to add additional acreage as it became available. The preserve includes two sandstone mounds jutting about 200 feet above dry forest and wetland terrain. Quincy Bluff, 2 miles long, lies to the west of a conifer swamp and shrubby wetland rich in rare plants. To the northeast, Lone Rock towers above a rumpled mixture of wetlands and forests, which closely recalls terrain of presettlement days.

Because of the preserve's size and the Conservancy's policy of permitting only activities that impact the land gently, you'll find no other hiking location in central Wisconsin that provides a more wilderness experience. You'll see few other hikers and no mountain bikes, all-terrain vehicles, or horses. But you might very well see a northern harrier hawk soaring overhead or hear the throaty call of a sandhill crane in the distance. The rare blue karner butterfly may also survive here, according to the Conservancy.

Description and special features. Two major trails penetrate the preserve. A network of about 5 miles of trails goes around, atop, and over a pass between higher portions of Quincy Bluff. Around and on the bluff it goes through oak and pine forest. It follows the wetland bordering the east side of the bluff.

A second trail goes for about 2 miles over ancient oak, aspen, and pine-covered sand ridges and around wetlands to Lone Rock. The trail climbs the sandstone mound to offer a wide view of the surrounding flatlands that were once the bed of Glacial Lake Wisconsin.

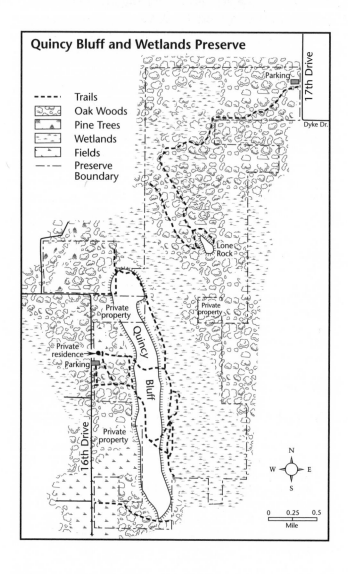

Quincy Bluff and Wetlands Preserve

Legend:
- - - - - Trails
- Oak Woods
- Pine Trees
- Wetlands
- Fields
- · — Preserve Boundary

17th Drive

Parking

Dyke Dr.

Lone Rock

Private property

Private property

Quincy Bluff

Private residence →

Parking

16th Drive

Private property

N
W · E
S

0   0.25   0.5
Mile

Degree of difficulty. Trails are generally wide, with a natural sandy soil surface. The Quincy Bluff trail tends to be steep on the side of the bluff and rocky in places. The Lone Rock trail goes over an undulating surface with only mild inclines until it reaches Lone Rock, where the slopes increase dramatically.

How to get there. Quincy Bluff: About 9 miles south of Adams on State Highway 13, go west on County Highway H for 2.3 miles to Sixteenth Avenue, then north 0.5 mile to Evergreen Avenue, then west 0.5 mile to Sixteenth Drive, then north 2.2 miles to the parking lot on the right.

Lone Rock: From County Highway F southwest of Adams, take Fourteenth Drive south 1.1 miles to a small parking lot on the right. This access is on DNR land.

Regulations. The Nature Conservancy prohibits the following in its preserves: pets (except seeing-eye dogs), horses, bicycles, all-terrain vehicles, camping or picnic fires, rock climbing or spelunking, fishing or trapping, and hunting except by special permission. Cleated hiking boots are discouraged. The Conservancy cautions against trespassing on private property adjoining the preserve.

Facilities. Parking.

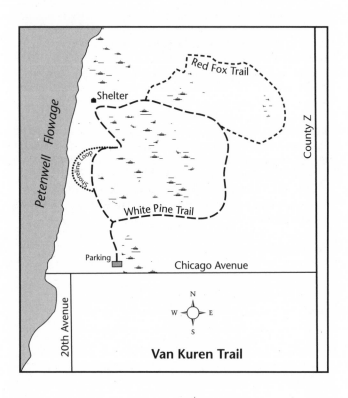

Petenwell Flowage

Red Fox Trail

Shelter

Shoreline Loop

White Pine Trail

County Z

Parking

Chicago Avenue

20th Avenue

N
W   E
S

Van Kuren Trail

3 Power Company's Trail Offers a Gentle Hiking Experience

Van Kuren Trail, Town of Strongs Prairie

The federally granted license to operate the Petenwell Dam on the Wisconsin River requires the power company to provide a land-use and recreation plan for the waters and surrounding land. As part of their plan, the Wisconsin River Power Company has built the Van Kuren Trail for cross-country skiing and hiking on wooded property next to the 23,000-acre Petenwell Flowage.

Description and special features. The 2.7-mile trail forms three loops, a main loop and a secondary loop branching out from the main one, over gently undulating terrain. A short side loop goes along the shore of the flowage. The wide, naturally surfaced trail winds through woods of oak, aspen, a few maples, and many large white pines. It also goes around a cattail marsh.

Interpretative signs along the trail identify species of trees and other highlights.

Degree of difficulty. Generally, the trail goes up and down over gentle, short slopes. I found only one steep incline, and a sign marked its location. On a sunny, late October day, small blue signs affixed to trees helped me follow the leaf-covered route.

How to get there. From its junction with State Highway 21 in western Adams County, take County Highway Z north 2 miles to Chicago Avenue, then west 0.7 mile to a parking lot on the right.

Regulations. No motor vehicles or camping are permitted. Users are asked to pack out any refuse.

Facilities. Parking is available. On a hill on the main trail, a shelter with fire ring and split logs overlooks the flowage. Bring your own kindling and matches.

Other points of interest in area

The power company has opened selected portions of its east dike for hiking, fishing, and wildlife observation. A hiking trail goes along the dike and through the Petenwell Wildlife Area. Park at the north end of Twenty-first Avenue.

Juneau County

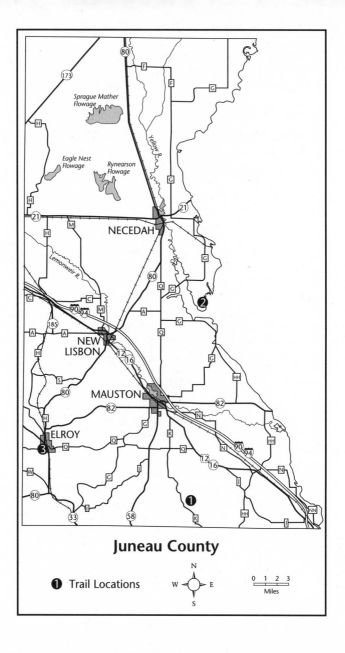

Juneau County

1 Trail Locations

N
W ⊕ E
S

0 1 2 3
Miles

1 Trail into a Deep Hollow an Unexpected Delight

Bass Hollow Recreation Area, southern Juneau County

When seeking out new hiking trails for this book, every so often I'd come upon an out-of-the-way path that's unexpectedly unique in an otherwise commonplace location. Bass Hollow is such a place. From the edge of a quiet little rural park, I hiked a trail that descends deeply into the heart of a fern-lined glen. In May, bright splashes of wild geraniums and colonies of trilliums bloomed on every side as tiny Sevenmile Creek cut its way into a V-shaped channel. However, "it's best in the fall because there are so many maples," says Dale Dorow, Juneau County forest and parks administrator.

Description and special features. From a recreation area along County K, a spur descends to a clearing. A 3-mile loop trail begins and ends there. Much of the trail goes through a climax forest, which may be old growth, according to Dorow. After a long descent, the trail follows the bank of the creek and crosses it. You will encounter a second clearing about a third of the way along the loop. There is a spur from this clearing, which I did not follow. Maples, basswoods, birches, oaks, and large-tooth aspens are among the many varieties of trees surrounding the trail. A chorus of birds, most of them unseen, provided background music during my springtime hike.

Degree of difficulty. Though about 6 feet wide in most places, the trail is rugged. The natural, mostly bare turf will be muddy in places during wet weather. I encountered standing water several days after a heavy rain. Some of the steep slopes are slippery when wet, and the long climb out of the hollow requires endurance.

How to get there. From the junction of U.S. Highway 12 and County K just south of Mauston, take K south 8 miles to the park on the left.

Regulations. The trail is open the year around but not plowed in winter. While cross-country skiing is allowed, I would rate it as very difficult. Dogs must be leashed on the trail and in the recreation area. No all-terrain vehicles are permitted. Dorow cautions hikers that hunters also use Bass Hollow.

Facilities. The recreation area has pit toilets, a pump, a picnic shelter, playground equipment, and parking.

Other points of interest in area

On the shore of the Petenwell Flowage at Eighth Street East sits another Juneau County facility, *Wilderness Park*. At this writing the county planned to expand it to 250 acres so that hiking trails will connect with old logging roads in a 7,000-acre county forest. For the current status of the expansion, phone Juneau County Forestry and Parks Department: 608-847-9390.

2 State Park Built on Flowage Peninsula

Buckhorn State Park, southeast of Necedah

In 1950 when the Wisconsin River was dammed just south of the Yellow River, a peninsula formed in the flowage where the Yellow and the Wisconsin had joined. The state acquired the land for a 3,000-acre park that's divided into a developed park and a wildlife area. Buckhorn offers several hiking trails and a wide variety of other activities, including wilderness camping, canoeing on a special interpretive trail, and turkey hunting.

Description and special features. Three trails, which are joined, can be reached from the south picnic area. All three thread through the wildlife area, which includes wetlands, oak and pine woods, a small prairie, and the Castle Rock Flowage shoreline.

The Nature Trail, 1.4 miles long, has about 30 interpretive stations to keep you tuned for signs of wildlife on the trail. Portions of the trail follow the flowage shoreline and go around a grassy marsh.

The Turkey Hollow Trail segment, 1.5 miles, passes a portion of the wilderness campground and goes deeper into the wildlife area.

The Partridge Trail, 1.2 miles long and opened in 1992, is used by small-game hunters as well as hikers. It is also accessible from a parking lot reserved for hunters during the fall hunting season.

Degree of difficulty. Terrain in the park is flat, and wood chips have been used liberally for paving to provide an easy walking experience. Several sturdy wooden bridges cross small streams, and a boardwalk traverses a shoreline wetland.

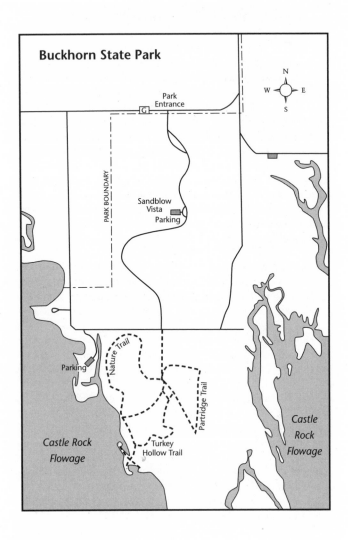

Buckhorn State Park

Park Entrance

G

PARK BOUNDARY

Sandblow
Vista
Parking

N
W · E
S

Parking

Nature Trail

Partridge Trail

Turkey
Hollow Trail

Castle Rock
Flowage

Castle
Rock
Flowage

How to get there. From the junction of State Highways 80 and 21 in Necedah, take 21 east 1 mile to County G, and take G south 8.6 miles to the park entrance on the left.

Regulations. The park is open to day users from 6:00 A.M. to 11:00 P.M. Bikes are not permitted, and dogs must be leashed on trails except when used for hunting. You will need a state park annual or daily permit for your auto.

Facilities. Restrooms and parking are available in the south picnic area, and a portable toilet is stationed in the wilderness campground near the Turkey Hollow Trail. This full-service state park offers an exceptionally wide variety of recreational activities. In addition to those mentioned above, there are a swimming beach, picnic shelters, playground equipment, group camping, horseshoes, volleyball, and, of course, fishing in the flowage.

Other points of interest in area

Sandblow Vista, a scenic overlook in the park, highlights an unusually large sandblow. Formed of sand that once occupied the bed of a huge postglacial lake, the barren surface supports little vegetation. According to a park staff person, early settlers attempted to farm the area that is now the park, but the sparse, porous sand proved to be poor farm land.

3 Elroy's the Hub for Biking, Hiking Trails

Elroy-Sparta State Park Trail, "400" State Trail, Omaha Trail, Elroy

Once a prominent railroad center, the southwest Juneau County community of Elroy now is a trailhead for three biking-hiking trails that follow the abandoned railroad beds. The city has built a downtown commons on old railroad property to service the needs of trail users.

Description and special features. Three trails totaling some 66 miles in length can be reached from the commons.

Elroy-Sparta State Park Trail. Thirty-two miles long, the trail passes through the "Hidden Valley" communities of Kendall, Wilton, and Norwalk on its way to Sparta. The trail is nationally known for the three rock tunnels it goes through, one of which is 0.75 mile long.

The "400" State Trail. Sandstone bluffs, many of which were islands in a huge lake that covered central Wisconsin in early postglacial times, delight users on this trail. Following the Baraboo River for 22 miles, the trail passes through the communities of La Valle, Wonewoc, and Union Center on its route between Reedsburg and Elroy.

The Omaha Trail. The only trail of the three located entirely within Juneau County and under its jurisdiction opened in 1992. Its asphalt paving makes it wheelchair friendly. The trail's 12.5-mile route passes through the village of Hustler and an 875-foot tunnel between Elroy and Camp Douglas.

Degree of difficulty. Packed limestone screenings pave the Elroy-Sparta and "400" trails, and asphalt paves the Omaha. Grades up to 3 percent (usually much less) on these old railroad beds make biking or hiking easy. Wooden planks have replaced steel tracks on bridges crossing rivers and streams, and wooden railings have been added.

How to get there. Elroy is in southwestern Juneau County where State Highways 71, 80, and 82 meet. You may enter trails in any of the communities along their routes.

Regulations. While both state and county trails require annual or day-use passes for bicyclists, hikers may use them free of charge. Carry a flashlight in tunnels. Tunnels on the Elroy-Sparta Trail are closed from November 15 to April 15.

Facilities. All trails have rest stops, some of which include restrooms, along their routes. In the Elroy Commons I found advertising publications containing a wealth of information about retailers, restaurants, campgrounds, and even emergency phone numbers in trail communities.

Other points of interest in area

Across State Highway 71 from the Elroy-Sparta State Park Trail parking lot on the western edge of Elroy, *Thompson Lake Park* has walking trails around the lake and to a campground on top of a hill. The view from the top is worth the climb.

Marquette County

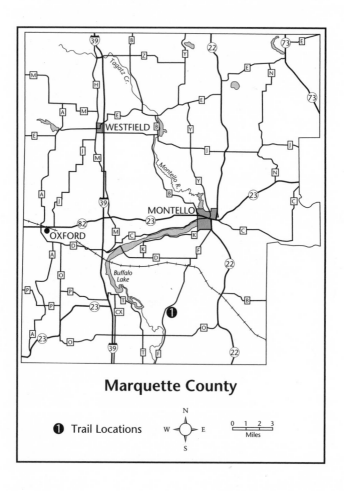

Marquette County

1 Trail Locations

N
W ⊕ E
S

0 1 2 3
Miles

1 Footpath Circles Lake at Naturalist Muir's Boyhood Home

John Muir Memorial Park, south of Montello

Muir, with his father and brother, came from Scotland to farm this glacial meadow by the lake in 1849. With all the curiosity and enthusiasm of an adolescent, he learned about the birds and flowers, the frogs and fish, of his new home. "Oh, that glorious Wisconsin wilderness!" he later wrote (*The Boyhood of a Naturalist,* 1913, p. 13). "Everything new and pure in the very prime of the spring when Nature's pulses were beating highest and mysteriously keeping time with our own."

Description and special features. Circling Ennis Lake, the path goes through a 150-acre state natural area and county park. Starting near County F at the south border of the park clearing, it goes through oak openings, woodlands, and sedge meadows. It skirts a lakeside fen and wet-mesic prairie, and several spurs lead to the tops of small hills. Muir's farm fields, now a prairie undergoing restoration, sparkled with an array of blooming thistles, asters, and other summer flowers during my July walk. The path returns to the park clearing on its north side after about 2.5 miles.

Degree of difficulty. Unsurfaced except for a small portion with crushed rock at the south trailhead, the trail becomes progressively narrow as it enters the sedge meadow on the south side of the lake. While steel guideposts show the way, portions of the path go through tall marsh grass on the south and north sides of the lake. The surface is firm near the lake, but it also may be wet. Wooden bridges cross the outlet stream several times. Slopes in lakeside woods are not steep. Because of the marshy portions of the trail, I recommend that you wear hiking boots rather than sneakers.

How to get there. From its intersection with State Highway 22, take County O west 4.3 miles to County F, and take F north 1.4

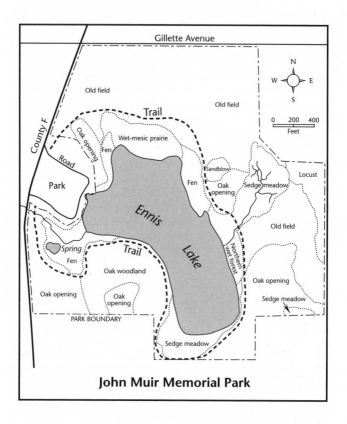

John Muir Memorial Park

miles to the park on the right. Or from its intersection with 22 in Montello, take F south 7.6 miles to the park on the left.

Regulations. Park hours are 4:00 A.M. to 10:00 P.M. Fishing in Ennis Lake requires a state license. No boat motors are allowed. You may cross-country ski, but the trail is not groomed.

Facilities. There are parking, pit toilets, picnic tables, a boat launch, and a pier.

Other points of interest in area

About 3 miles from the park off Gillette Avenue, a rustic path goes through a state natural area to the top of *Observatory Hill,* which is mentioned in Muir's writings. The undeveloped property is not marked, and the path is steep and hard to follow. It is not a state-designated trail. Hikers use it at their own risk.

Waushara County

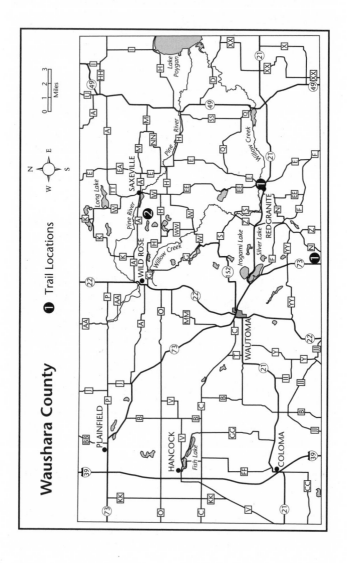

Waushara County

● Trail Locations

1 Trail Follows Route of Granite-Hauling Railroad

Bannerman Trail, Redgranite

Early farmers near Sand Prairie in southeastern Waushara County discovered that the hard, red rock of many outcroppings was a high grade of granite. The quarried rock was especially good for street paving. Local citizens prospered as the rock became king. They even renamed their community Redgranite. The Chicago and Northwestern Railroad built a spur linking the quarries so the rock could be hauled to Chicago. Eventually concrete and asphalt replaced paving rock, and the railroad was abandoned.

Redgranite, however, was born again as a thriving tourist center, with the local quarry as one of many attractions. The bed of the railroad spur is now a 7-mile hiking and snowmobile trail.

Description and special features. From a trailhead on County E near downtown Redgranite, the trail goes southwest through the hamlets of Lohrville and Spring Lake. A 1-mile-plus segment from Spring Lake to the southwest, to where the trail crosses County N, goes through operating farms and is not open to hikers during the growing season. Hikers should follow N more or less parallel to the trail route until the trail crosses the road, then continue on the trail. The trail ends at a parking lot on State Highway 73, 0.1 mile north of Czech Avenue.

The route goes through a number of deciduous woodlands as well as farm land. It passes two quarries, which are now part of the Waushara County park system.

Degree of difficulty. A level, natural surface makes for easy walking.

How to get there. Redgranite is in southeastern Waushara County. The Highway 73 trailhead is 4.7 miles south of 73's junction with State Highway 21 in Wautoma.

Regulations. The trail is open from 5:30 A.M. to 10:30 P.M. during the hiking season. Dogs must be leashed. No motor vehicles, except snowmobiles, are allowed.

Facilities. You may park in the lot at the Highway 73 trailhead or at Flynn's Quarry on County N, 2 miles southwest of Redgranite. In Redgranite, park on the street. There is a pit toilet at Flynn's Quarry.

Other points of interest in area

Along the trail in Lohrville, the stone quarry has been developed into the unique *West Point Dive Park.* The Inland Seas Diving Academy leases the 45-foot-deep quarry lake and provides scuba diving lessons there. Phone 414-722-0051 for information. A new hiking trail has been built in this 40-acre park, much of which is wooded.

2 Nature Trail Loops through Pine Plantation

Kusel Lake County Park, Saxeville

Red and white pines tower above the self-guiding nature trail in this quiet lakeside park. It's a place where you might want to picnic, play tennis, or watch your children on playground swings.

Description and special features. A wide looping trail goes for about a mile through a pine plantation. Information stations along the way identify the trees, plants, and wildlife. For cross-country skiers, two longer loops branch off the nature trail and go through mildly hilly terrain.

Degree of difficulty. With a thick blanket of wood chips in many places, the trail surface tends to be soft but not difficult. The forest provides cool shade on a hot summer day. There are a few gentle slopes near the lakeshore.

How to get there. From Saxeville take County A west 1.8 miles to Twenty-fourth Avenue, then south 0.9 mile to the park entrance on the right.

Regulations. Open hours are 5:30 A.M. to 10:30 P.M. Dogs must be leashed. Cross-country skiing is permitted.

Facilities. This well-equipped park has restrooms, picnic shelters and grills, playground equipment, tennis courts, a swimming beach, and a boat launch.

Other points of interest in area

See how the Department of Natural Resources grows fish for stocking at the fish hatchery in the village of Wild Rose, 4.5 miles east of Kusel Lake on County A. The hatchery complex raises brown trout, chinook salmon, muskie, and northern pike. Visitors may tour daily from 8:00 A.M. to 4:00 P.M.

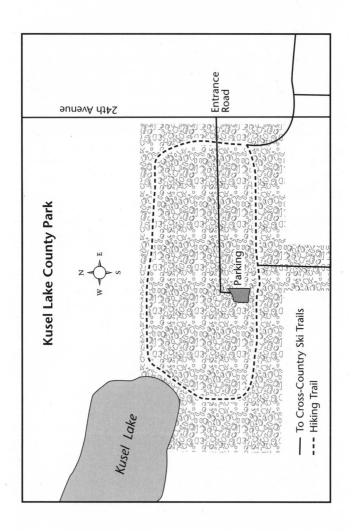

Kusel Lake County Park

24th Avenue

Entrance Road

Parking

Kusel Lake

N
W   E
S

—— To Cross-Country Ski Trails
-- -- Hiking Trail

Reference Material

Trails and Walking Places of Historical or Archaeological Significance

Bannerman Trail This trail follows the bed of an old railroad that carried granite rock from several quarries to Redgranite.
Pp. 264–66

Berlin Historical Neighborhood Tours Two walking tours showcase nineteenth-century homes built by New England and New York settlers.
Pp. 37–38

Houdini Historic Walking Tour This urban tour highlights events in the life of the famous Appleton illusionist.
Pp. 43–45

John Muir Memorial Park The "Father of the National Park System" learned about nature and wildlife on a farm his family homesteaded on this Marquette County site.
Pp. 258–61

Ken Euers Nature Area A walking trail through a Green Bay coastal wetland provides insights into the natural and human history of the area.
Pp. 10–12

Lasley Point Archaeological Site Between A.D. 1200 and 1500 a village of Oneota Indians lived on this site near Lake Poygan.
Pp. 57–58

Marshfield Historical Walking Tour After a 1887 fire, Marshfield businessmen rebuilt with brick. Many of those buildings remain today and can be seen on this tour.
Pp. 220–21

Milwaukee Historical Building Tours Walking tours among the city's architectural treasures reflect its ethnic roots.
Pp. 139–41

Newport State Park Nineteenth-century settlers cleared a virgin forest and tried to farm the land. Park trails trace the remains of their efforts. Pp. 71–73

Old Plank Road Trail Pioneers followed an Indian path when they built a plank road from Sheboygan to Greenbush. Now an asphalt-paved trail borders State Highway 23 over the same route. Pp. 122–24

The Ridges Sanctuary The cyclical rise and fall of the level of Lake Michigan formed the ridges in this first of Wisconsin's designated natural areas. Pp. 82–84

Washington Avenue Historic District Cedarburg boomed when the railroad came in 1870. Citizens built a variety of structures you can view on this walking tour. Pp. 146–48

Whitefish Dunes State Park Archaeologists have discovered at least eight stages of occupation of this site over the past 2,000 years. Pp. 85–88

Trails and Walking Places with Prominent Ice Age Features

Bark River Segment, Ice Age Trail, meanders through bottom-lands of the Bark River, which is a remnant of a giant spillway formed by the melting glacier. Pp. 164–66

Glacier Hills County Park in southern Washington County sits atop the kettle moraine. Four trails offer moraine hiking, and you can swim in a glacially formed lake. Pp. 156–59

Horicon Marsh Wildlife Area is a unit of Wisconsin's Ice Age National Scientific Reserve. It was included here because it is an outstanding example of an extinct postglacial lake.
Pp. 180–86

Kettle Moraine State Forest, Northern Unit, preserves a major portion of the unique kettle moraine region formed between two lobes of the great glacier. Classic kettles, kames, eskers, and other landforms can be seen as you hike the trails here. Pp. 110–15

Potawatomi State Park contains several examples ancient shorelines of postglacial lakes, predecessors of Lake Michigan. The eastern trailhead of the Ice Age National Scenic Trail is located in this park. Pp. 79–81

Riveredge Nature Center, near eastern Wisconsin's kettle moraine region, has a kame within its boundaries. Pp. 149–53

Sandhill Wildlife Area lies within Glacial Lake Wisconsin, a huge lake formed in what is now central Wisconsin by run-off from the melting glacier. It is believed the lake suddenly drained, with rushing water forming the colorful rocky gorges of the Wisconsin Dells. Pp. 227–29

Waupaca-Portage Counties Segment, Ice Age Trail, goes through Emmons Creek Fish and Wildlife Area and Hartman Creek State Park, over drumlins and by kettles.   Pp. 211–13

West Bend Segment, Ice Age Trail, follows high moraines and eskers formed by the Lake Michigan lobe of the glacier.

Pp. 160–61

Trails and Walking Places with Picnic Areas and Playgrounds

Hiking can be an adventure of discovery for children. If you have kids, you may want to take them with you to trails that have accompanying picnic areas and playgrounds, and make a day of it. The following are so equipped, and some also have swimming beaches.

Bass Hollow Recreation Area, pp. 248–50
Buckhorn State Park, pp. 251–53
Cherney Maribel Caves County Park, pp. 96–98
Glacier Hills County Park, pp. 156–59
Hartman Creek State Park, pp. 206–10
Henry R. Schuette Park, pp. 104–5
Jordan Park, pp. 198–200
Kohler-Andrae State Park, pp. 116–19
Kusel Lake County Park, pp. 267–68
Lake Park, pp. 142–43
Maywood, Evergreen, Jaycee Parks, pp. 120–21
Naga-Waukee Park, pp. 172–74
Memorial Park, Neenah pp. 59–60
Newport State Park, pp. 71–73
Peninsula State Park, pp. 74–78
Petenwell County Park, pp. 238–40
Plamann Park, pp. 49–50
Potawatomi State Park, pp. 79–81
Powers Bluff Park, pp. 222–24
River Park, pp. 125–26
South Wood County Park-Lake Wazeecha, pp. 230–31
Walla Hi County Park, p. 98
Whitefish Dunes State Park, pp. 85–88

Trails and Walking Places Where Cross-Country Skiing Is Allowed

Ahnapee State Trail, pp. 90–93
Bannerman Trail, pp. 264–66
Bass Hollow Recreation Area, pp. 248–50
Bay Beach Wildlife Sanctuary, pp. 5–6
Brillion Wildlife Area, pp. 15–18
Buckhorn State Park, pp. 251–53
Bugline Recreation Trail, pp. 167–69
Cofrin Arboretum, pp. 7–9
Consolidated Papers Forest Tour, pp. 216–19
Glacier Hills County Park, pp. 156–59
Gordon Bubolz Nature Preserve, pp. 41–42
Green Circle, pp. 194–97
Hartman Creek State Park, pp. 206–10
Havenwoods State Forest, pp. 136–38
Henry R. Schuette Park, pp. 104–5
High Cliff State Park, pp. 19–22
Hobbs Woods Nature Area, pp. 29–31
Horicon Marsh, pp. 180–86
John Muir Memorial Park, pp. 258–61
Jordan Park, pp. 198–200
Kettle Moraine State Forest, pp. 110–15
Kohler-Andrae State Park, pp. 116–19
Kusel Lake County Park, pp. 267–68
Lasley Point Archaeological Site, pp. 57–58
Ledge View Nature Center, pp. 23–26
Maywood, Evergreen, Jaycee Parks, pp. 120–21
Newport State Park, pp. 71–73
Nepco Lake County Park, p. 231
Old Plank Road Trail, pp. 122–24
Peninsula State Park, pp. 74–78
Petenwell County Park, pp. 238–40
Plamann Park, pp. 49–50
Point Beach State Forest, pp. 101–103
Potawatomi State Park, pp. 79–81
Powers Bluff Park, pp. 222–24

Index of Trails and Walking Places